# PROFIT FROM EXHIBITIONS
# AND TRADE FAIRS

# PROFIT FROM EXHIBITIONS AND TRADE FAIRS

Alan Taylor, MCIM

2000

First published in 1995 by Management Books 2000 Ltd
125a The Broadway, Didcot, Oxfordshire OX11 8AW

Printed and bound in Great Britain by
WBC, Bridgend, Mid Glam.

*British Library Cataloguing in Publication Data is available*

ISBN 1-85252-200-3

# CONTENTS

# Contents

# Contents

# INTRODUCTION

The need for a more informed and professional approach to exhibitions and exhibiting is greater now than ever as manufacturers struggle to recover from a recession that, although worldwide, has been particularly severe in the UK.

The value of exhibitions is frequently not understood by marketing departments which fail to capitalise on the unique opportunity they present. They are occasions when the customer comes to your door seeking information which a sales representative cannot always give, and if properly manned your team will include top technical personnel to provide instant in-depth back-up.

I believe many companies fail to capitalise on the opportunities available when exhibiting due to lack of preparation so that staff have no clear-cut ideas of how they should deal with enquiries. If by reading this book you are able to take a more informed and professional approach to exhibiting then the author's time will have been well spent.

Alan Taylor's book takes the reader through each stage of exhibiting, a 'hands-on' guide that helps you make the right decisions. The advice and knowledge available have been learnt the hard way, for Alan's pedigree is impeccable, having served his apprenticeship through a lifetime of service to the exhibition industry.

*Peter Cole,* Editor, *Exhibition Bulletin*

# FOREWORD

In Britain, exhibitions have gained greatly in stature and reputation since the NEC opened in 1976. In European terms, the entrepreneurial market-led approach adopted by UK organisers has won considerable respect. Alan Taylor has played an important part in injecting innovation into British-based exhibitions.

The quality of exhibition facilities has also been transformed. Venues throughout the country have been modernised and the NEC, Birmingham, has been able to respond to each stage of additional demand for display space, growing from 89,000 square metres in 1976 to 158,000 square metres in 1994. It is now one of Europe's premier showplaces. Alan Taylor contributed much to our initial design process and the transfer of major trade fairs to the National Exhibition Centre.

*T E Golding,* Chief Executive, National Exhibition Centre

I have known Alan Taylor for over 40 years, initially as a stand builder and later as a manager and director of companies within the Montgomery Group, a major international exhibition organiser. The knowledge gained by Alan will no doubt produce a book that will not only be a Bible for the new recruit but an essential 'aide-memoire' for the seasoned professional.

The low profile always adopted by Alan may have made him less known than perhaps some others within the industry. It should not, however, be overlooked that his introduction of the aluminium framed Shell-Scheme system at 'Interbuild' in 1975 was the forerunner to its adoption by exhibition organisers for perhaps 99 per cent of current use.

*A W Francis*, Consultant

# PROLOGUE

My life in exhibitions and trade fairs started by accident in 1948. Two years earlier I had been demobilised from the RAF after wartime service which had taken me to many countries and left me very restless. In those two years I had tried to resume my intended career in building management, but by comparison with wartime life it seemed painfully dull, not something I wanted to do for my entire working life!

Quite by chance, I was introduced to the world of exhibitions and immediately decided that was to be my future career. I had been told that my earlier background in construction could be useful. I considered myself most fortunate when I was accepted as a junior executive in the production department of the City Display Organisation (CDO) – at that time the foremost exhibition group in the UK, numbering many top manufacturers and world governments amongst its clientele. My job was to assist highly skilled people to progress contracts through the workshops onto site – wherever that was to be – and generally learn the exhibition business.

It was an exciting time. The country was looking forward to the 1951 Festival of Britain and much of it was being discussed, planned and prefabricated at CDO. Architects and designers were visiting the directors and senior executives daily. Models and visuals of their various projects were being examined and developed. Basil Spence (as he was then) was to be seen checking details and helping in the construction of his magnificent model of the new Coventry Cathedral in the model shop, while other projects were to be seen in prototype or model form or being prefabricated in the workshops.

There was much to learn and like many others I was in a hurry to advance my career. I wanted to play a fuller part. At that time, I hadn't decided which area of the business attracted me most. The choice had to be made from the five categories that make up all exhibitions and trade fairs: clients/exhibitors, organiser, designer/architect, stand builder and associated contractors or hall/venue manager. This choice could be made later when I had more knowledge of the subject. It was more important that I found answers to the immediate mysteries on which I was currently engaged.

It seemed logical to seek help from the 'old-timers' – those who always knew how to interpret a difficult drawing or specification or how to clarify an intricate brief. I was very naive – 'know-how' spelt better jobs and faster promotion. No way were they going to share this with a newcomer! It seemed that books had to be the way that I was going to find the answers, but once again I was wrong. There were none in existence that dealt with the total exhibition scenario as it was then.

Some interesting books reviewing exhibition design were available; one by Beverley Pick still stays in my mind as the most comprehensive, which illustrated and explained the design trends of the day. Several interesting histories existed from which I learnt that Leipzig has the oldest known 'trade fair' and that the tinkers and merchants travelling around the market places and goose fairs in Britain in the Middle Ages must have been the first exhibitors in this country (the Chinese and Egyptians were busy centuries earlier), thus making the farmers or landowners the first venue owners! No book, however, provided the answers that I and many others were seeking – how to evaluate, estimate or to prepare a script or brief, to name but some of the essentials that an 'exhibition innocent' needed to know.

In the build-up to the Festival of Britain, like many others I was thrown in at the deep end and told to get on with it. The

South Bank, Skylon and Battersea Park became very real to me – this was my training ground and I was very much the rookie learning the trade. By the time work was due to be started on one of the last attractions, 'The Festival of Faith' at St Paul's cathedral crypt, I found myself working alone under the kindly guidance of the designer. It was then I realised I was totally hooked on this odd business.

Since then I have travelled to many parts of the world involved in similar events from Afrifoods, staged in Morocco in 1974, through to my last public exhibition, Riyadh – Yesterday and Today, at Olympia in 1986. In between times, trade fairs took me to many parts of Europe, Africa, Asia and America. Although the actual building of exhibitions was my first love, organisation has taken far more of my time so I now know which of the five elements of exhibitions interests me most. Now more than forty years on, having enjoyed an interesting life and been associated at some time or another with all of those five categories and listened many times to those same questions that had puzzled me, it seemed time that a comprehensive exhibition book was produced explaining without waffle or mystique how these various aspects of exhibitions and trade fairs work.

Many new firms discover trade exhibitions every year: if one accepts current figures, there are about 70,000 exhibitors every year. There is no great mystique – exhibitions and trade fairs rely on logic and common sense. I have endeavoured to explain how the different aspects work, how they come together and what skills are needed. There can be no doubt that exhibitions and trade fairs will continue to excite people's imagination and interest even though other forms of promotion will undoubtedly develop. Chatting to others in the same field of business is a natural instinct – it's been happening for years and will continue to do so, even in this sophisticated age we have arrived at. Where better to do this than at an exhibition?

As new companies decide to exhibit, they will require answers to questions that never occurred to them before – as happened to me in 1948. I hope this book will cast some light.

# ACKNOWLEDGEMENTS

I count myself fortunate in being taught my craft by a very gifted entrepreneur: Fred Keil, who founded City Display Organisation and developed exhibition techniques unthought of by existing builders in 1946-48 after the Second World War. These methods were very soon being followed by exhibition companies both in the UK and continental Europe. As well as learning many different and distinctive new ideas and procedures, I had the opportunity of meeting top designers of the period. Learning how to attract and use all manner of techniques to interest an audience became second nature in this 'exhibition university'. I acknowledge Fred Keil's great influence on my life in exhibitions.

Many old colleagues from the Montgomery Group have helped in providing material and recalling incidents for this book. In particular I should like to acknowledge Peter Lendrum, Michael Berger and Viv Caisey for their help in locating photographs and references. Mike Agostini in his inimitable way provided literary logic and Peter Cole from *Exhibition Bulletin* provided much practical help. My friend of many years' standing, Arthur Francis, reminded me of matters 'stand-fitting'.

I also thank Terry Golding and John Cole from the NEC for their help in points of detail, Guy Nissen of the DTI for his invaluable help on export facts and figures, and Reg Best of ISBA for providing exhibition and trade fair facts; Paul Lee of

RT Displays for his great help in providing the latest details on modular systems. John Glanfield and Teresa Lunn of Earls Court/Olympia provided photographs and memories of the places of past triumphs. Finally, but not least, my grateful thanks to my wife Winifred, who has tolerated my irregular exhibition working hours and unexpected travel arrangements with so much humour and understanding over the years.

*The Grand Hall Olympia, designed by the Architect Henry E. Coe, was opened in 1886. Since then Olympia has expanded but the famous roof, which spans 170 feet (51.8 metres), remains unchanged. At its highest point it is 100 feet (30.5 metres) above the ground.*

# 1

# REASONS TO EXHIBIT AND TYPES OF EXHIBITION

A company must have good reasons to exhibit, otherwise it cannot plan a strategy that will benefit itself or the exhibition. Therefore the first question it must consider is whether or not it really does want to exhibit.

It is neither easy nor cheap to stage a worthwhile and successful exhibition stand. As a project, it can be a frustrating experience. Yet exhibitions can be very rewarding when the planning and time spent prove to be successful and trade buyers demonstrate their approval by the enquiries they place with stand staff. At a public show orders are usually made directly on the exhibition stand, and more immediate reaction will be seen. Trade fair stand enquiries generally require more time for processing and the results are not so immediate.

## OBJECTIVES

Exhibitions and trade fairs are part of the marketing process. They have advantages which other forms of marketing and promotions cannot offer. They provide the opportunity for large numbers of buyers and sellers in an industry to come into direct contact with each other in one place at the same time. Products of interest to the buyers can be viewed at the time that discussion is taking place, allowing the opportunity to handle, examine and compare with other products, go away to examine other companies' products and return again for further examination, all within a short space of time.

Very few other selling situations can offer this flexible facility. Where else, for example, can competitors' products be seen nearby, enabling instant visual comparison. New products can be displayed in premier positions supported by appropriate captioning, highlighted and signposted. Dominant displays inevitably attract the trade press as well as passing buyers. Such press attention can result in reviews of products in the relevant trade publications. As new technologies develop exhibitions and trade shows provide a splendid showcase and furnish opportunities unavailable to other media.

By their very nature exhibitions and trade fairs are very public. The efficient company is seen to be so while the inefficient will not make a favourable impression. Smaller companies can take advantage of the event by showing themselves to be well-organised operations. They do not need a large stand to do this: competent management combined with considerate and efficient staff will suffice.

Product research can also be undertaken at exhibitions and trade fairs since there is a ready-made audience of the very people who it is hoped will ultimately buy the product being researched. They may not even be known as customers but their views on new developments and ideas for restyling or improving existing products can be invaluable. They will also be flattered to be asked to provide an opinion on your new product – it could be the beginning of a blossoming relationship! Some specialised exhibitions are also accompanied by conferences. In such cases the cross-fertilisation between conference and exhibition offers particularly good opportunities for product research. A competent presenter should have little

*The visitor has the opportunity to touch, examine and compare the product whilst discussion is taking place. (Photograph courtesy of Interbuild Exhibitions and Apollo Photographers.)*

trouble ensuring that his stand is visited and the appropriate product sought.

Test marketing of new products can be carried out at exhibitions. If the product is not right and does not appeal to trade audiences at an exhibition this will very soon become apparent since visiting buyers will quickly see the advantages or disadvantages and react accordingly. In addition, this research can provide an indication of the likely production run needed for any new product.

Well publicised launches of new products often attract interest from competitors as well as the press. In such cases it may sometimes be necessary to restrict the viewing opportunities with a suitably modified display treatment.

Exhibitors expect to meet old customers and friends. This is one purpose of an exhibition, but it also provides an opportunity for the visiting buyer to be introduced to other executives and employees whom he does not normally meet – for example, the research manager or the sales office manager or others who share in providing the product the customer ultimately buys. The customer has to deal with these people – usually at the end of a telephone – and it can be useful for both buyer and seller to get to know each other better. Such meetings lead to better understanding and possibly increased business. Certainly it provides another contact.

A major contribution of exhibitions is to provide the opportunity to meet different buyers. Both buyer and seller can use
the event to update their knowledge of the other. People new to
an industry often use exhibitions to familiarise themselves with
other companies, processes and people in their area. It is an
effective method of achieving this objective; by asking questions of the stand representative a visiting buyer or specifier can
build a clear impression of a company (though perhaps not
always the image the company and its management would wish
for!).

It is important that stand representatives should always
initially establish the name, company and interest of the person
to whom they are speaking. Courtesy and good manners
demand it, and also too much information is often freely given
to competitors because careless and inexperienced stand staff
did not know to whom they were speaking.

The opening or VIP day is usually a social event at which
the company chairman and other directors take the opportunity
of fraternising with their opposite numbers and meet ministers,
MPs and other personalities who might be present. These occasions are well patronised by the media since this is the industry
get-together where a careless or ill-considered comment or a
hint of gossip could well be magnified, sometimes out of all
proportion, in the next issue of an influential publication. More
positively, useful joint ventures are often started as a result of a
casual conversation at such events.

## EXHIBITING FOR THE RIGHT REASONS

Having decided to exhibit it is necessary to establish your
prime reasons for showing. These might be to:

- Introduce goods, products or services.
- Demonstrate goods, products or services.
- Research goods, products or services.
- Test market products.

- Meet old and new customers.
- Enter new export markets.
- Support trade associations.
- Above all, to sell more products profitably.

Now it is also necessary to decide which exhibition or trade show you will support. In many industries there are maybe one or two main trade shows, whilst in others there may be several to choose from. Trade associations can provide useful data to help in the choice. All exhibitions and trade shows also produce information relating to attendance, numbers of exhibitors – both national and international – and sometimes press cuttings.

Overseas exhibitions provide the back-up that export sales people need, particularly if their firm is new to that market. Indeed, many overseas exhibitions have been the springboard that launched an export salesperson into their first overseas order.

Government trade and industry departments provide much useful assistance and information for the first-time overseas exhibitor and should always be approached when considering an overseas trade fair. (Exhibiting overseas is discussed in Chapter 8 and Appendix 3 provides further information.)

Sometimes a trade association will ask its members to support a group presentation in the UK or overseas. If a good reason is provided for such a presentation, this can be advantageous since group stands are less expensive (particularly overseas) and can pay dividends. Certainly they provide good opportunities for social interchange, new contact names, new enquiries for products to be introduced and an opportunity to share in group brochures that could reach an important new trade audience.

## TYPES OF EXHIBITION

There are two basic categories of exhibition: trade and industrial fairs and consumer/public events.

The yearly exhibition lists always show more trade and industrial events than public or consumer shows. Manufacturers appealing to industry have to communicate with their customers somehow. This is usually through representatives or by correspondence, but face-to-face meetings provide the best environment for doing business. A trade show provides this opportunity and there is hardly an industry which does not now have its own exhibition or trade show. Exhibition organisers and trade associations spend a great deal of time in planning show dates that do not clash with other industry events around the world to ensure the best buying and specifying dates for the trade visitors.

## TRADE AND INDUSTRIAL FAIRS

Trade and industrial exhibitions and fairs fall into the following categories, whether in the UK or overseas:

- Trade fairs for a particular industry or related group.
- Travelling exhibitions for a group or one company. (Road vehicles, railway coaches, ships and large aircraft can be used for this purpose.)
- Hotel, universities and school exhibitions.
- Combined conferences and exhibitions.
- Company product launches
- Agricultural shows.

## CONSUMER AND PUBLIC EXHIBITIONS

Consumer shows are intended mainly to attract the public. They are staged in many ways and fall into several categories:

- Public exhibitions or 'spectaculars'.
- Garden festivals.
- Agricultural and flower shows.

- Department store exhibitions and promotions.
- Shopping arcade or precinct and leisure complex events.
- Local events such as carnivals and fetes

## COMPANY 'IN-HOUSE' EVENTS

These are often used as a method of recruitment for a local company. Prospective staff interviews can be conducted and the community introduced to a new company. They are more frequent at times of a strong economy when staff are in short supply.

## OTHER EXHIBITION/DISPLAY ATTRACTIONS

Department stores may use their windows and if they have an exhibition hall this can also be used to house manufacturers' promotions. For example, perfumery companies may arrange product promotions with quickly assembled travelling display stands. Such events can also be held in collaboration with the local newspaper.

Radio, television and video promotions can also be held in this manner. Cameras and associated equipment are products that lend themselves to this type of promotion. Cars are frequently displayed in shopping arcades and precincts. Special offers can also be made with these types of promotion. For example golf and sports clubs can use their grounds – especially in summer months – to encourage sporting goods manufacturers to display their products.

With the growing number of hypermarkets and shopping malls, the opportunity for expanding exhibition capacity will increase as greater numbers of people are attracted by the visual potential. The greater opportunity of choice and the ability to touch and examine the products will attract the public.

*The London Wine Trade Fair in the Grand Hall, Olympia. Wines are exhibited from every wine-producing country in the world. (Photograph courtesy of Press Office, Earls Court/Olympia.)*

## EXHIBITION AND TRADE FAIR DESIGNATION

Exhibitions are often described as 'International' or 'National' events. This designation was instituted by the Association of Exhibition Organisers. They state that the term 'international' should be applied only to an event that includes at least 10 per cent overseas exhibitors or attracts a significant number of registered overseas buyers. The AEO and the *Union des Foires Internationales* (UFI) monitor their member companies to ensure that high standards are maintained.

# 2

# PREPARING TO PARTICIPATE

Having made the decision to exhibit and chosen the relevant exhibition or trade show, the next step is to decide who is to be the exhibition manager – the person who will be responsible for making many important decisions on behalf of the company.

A recent survey suggests that although some £500 million is spent by approximately 70,000 companies every year (generally some 700 exhibitions and trade fairs are listed yearly in the UK with an average of 100 exhibitors participating in each) only about 200 or so of the larger companies employ a full-time exhibition manager – an alarming statistic for an industry attracting such a great number of buyers, not only from Britain but also overseas.

## THE EXHIBITION MANAGER

The exhibition manager clearly carries a great responsibility. He or she must be in total command and the final arbiter in all matters relating to the exhibition, with the authority to approach and negotiate with all concerned whether they be in-house executives or outside personnel. They must be recognised as the person who takes the ultimate decision.

Control of the stand and the budget must be their prime responsibility. If every person who is likely to come into contact with the stand builder is allowed to request additional items or alterations without consulting the exhibition manager the extra costs could undermine the project. Professional designers and contractors recognise that the exhibition manager has the final responsibility for all orders relating to the stand.

Since there are so few professional exhibition managers it is likely they must be chosen from the staff available. It is unlikely that personnel from sales, production or any similar department would have the time to devote to a major exhibition, and they cannot be expected to have the basic knowledge that is required. The choice is usually someone from the publicity or marketing department. The person must be senior enough to have the authority to approach heads of all departments that are likely to be involved throughout the company. In practice it could well be the assistant publicity manager since he or she will already know all the divisional managers and their products.

Once appointed, the exhibition manager (EM) must prepare a script (the image the company is endeavouring to project) which will be developed into the exhibition brief. To do this, the EM needs to consult all the department heads and ascertain their opinions, requirements and the space they wish to have in order to accommodate their requirements.

It is essential that the EM balances the requirements of the various departments in accordance with company policy and objectives. A great diversity of views will be found. The sales manager normally sees it as an opportunity to increase sales but will point out that the demand on sales representatives' time will cause problems; the works manager will mention difficulties in meeting the need for specially prepared models and any increased product demand created by the show, whilst the finance director may resist demands for increased expenditure. They will all consider their view to be correct, which is why it is essential to have the company chief executive supporting the choice of the person deputed for this role. It is the firm that will be on display and the projected image should favour the company.

## COLLECTING AND COLLATING INFORMATION

As an example, assume that senior management has decided that the stand will focus on 'New products', 'Research and development' and 'Improved service facilities'. It might also be the intention to introduce an entirely new division – if it is ready in time. The EM is often faced with this type of problem. Space has to be allocated in the initial planning but an alternative scenario has to be ready for substitution at short notice. More often than not, this takes the form of duplicating a popular product item already shown in one display or area.

All concerned, particularly the designer and builder, must have advance knowledge of any possible changes so they can plan accordingly. The initial script for larger trade shows will have been drafted some months ahead of the event. The EM must ensure that all items are documented as they arise, including any probable last-minute changes.

Many managers will request more space than necessary for their products. The EM must argue the point and establish a fair compromise. All space on the stand is costly in its finished exhibition form. After discussions with all concerned, he should prepare what he considers to be a fair appraisal of the total requirement. After calculating and preparing a realistic 'guesstimate' of office and general space the probable area will become apparent.

The minutes of the meetings should be issued to all those who participated in the formation of the script since they will form the basis of the final details, such as the size of space required for each division's products, the time needed to prepare exhibits and all other relevant details. From this an exhibition 'brief' can be formulated.

## SUGGESTED BUDGET FIGURE

Management's first question to the appointed EM when he submits his script will be, 'How much will this cost?'. The wise manager will have calculated a 'suggested' budget figure which will be qualified after the organisers have offered an appropriate stand and costing. Meanwhile he will also have approached known designers and gained an indication of the design fee together with the probable standfitting costs. These are usually quoted as a cost per square metre, which will vary according to the size and complexity of the envisaged stand. (Budget planning is dealt with in Chapter 4.) Management is likely to find many objections, such as: 'Do we need all this space?'; 'Is an office necessary?'; 'What is that division trying to do – wouldn't it be better to use the trade journal?'. Many objections can be encountered; it is the task of the EM to provide the answers to these questions.

Assuming the EM has overcome management's objections and the 'guesstimate' has been accepted, the script can now be converted into an exhibition brief for final approval and implementation, and a working programme can be established.

## EXHIBITION BRIEF AND PRELIMINARY TIMETABLE

The brief is the culmination of ideas, suggestions and requests by all concerned to arrive at a suitable exhibition stand. It contains all product details, including the size, weight, colour and power requirements of all products, preferably illustrated by brochures. It should indicate which are to be working exhibits and which need safety rails or other precautions. It indicates the order of exhibit importance so that the designer knows which are to receive greatest prominence. Captions and copy should be included and where the final caption detail is not known, an indication of the amount of copy should be provided (for example three paragraphs or 300 words). Slogans and headlines together with any associated colour and logo references should be made available.

The suggested number of 'selling stations' (depending on the product and stand size) should be suggested to the designer. The office, storeroom and entertaining area should also be noted.

Machinery exhibits often need time to 'bed in', while computers and some electronic equipment require 'clean' electrical points as well as an absolutely level base. The designer must know this, just as he needs to know the electrical energy demand and if it should be single- or three-phase power.

Many companies like floral decoration or have a preference for a particular style of furniture. The brief must convey this to the designer. If it is intended to provide refreshments in a lounge area appropriate arrangements for hot and cold water may have to be made to satisfy the requirements of the Health and Safety Executive. In preparing a brief it is customary, indeed essential, to start at the floor and progress upwards to the top. Nothing is then forgotten.

Some sites are better than others. Island sites are better for large self-standing exhibits while corner sites serve two aisles and can interest 'flows' from two directions.

Most briefings are written and then discussed face-to-face with the designer so that any nuances can be clarified. The brief usually contains six sections:

1. Site and show details
2. Exhibitors' general views
3. Definite requirements
4. Company particulars
5. Proposed budget
6. Timetable

After considering any comments made by the chosen designer, an appropriate stand site can be finalised with the exhibition or trade fair organisers. In the meantime, discussions can commence with the designer and a rough general visual of the proposed stand can be prepared.

## SAMPLE EXHIBITION BRIEF

*1. 'The Advanced Woodworking Machinery Trade show', 12-17 October 1995. Hall 6, The Exhibition Centre, London.*

Stand number not known at this stage but the exhibition organiser has assured us he will allocate a corner-sited stand with two open frontages as indicated on the floor-plan, measuring 25 × 18 metres to provide a total area of 450 square metres. The site will be 'space only', corner position and the longest side, 25 metres, will be located on a major aisle while the 18-metre side will be on gangway that leads to a bar. Copy of exhibition rules and regulations attached.

*2. General view.* We are proposing to display our range of wood-working machinery as the brochures attached illustrate. Three models are available, ABI10, ABI11 and ABI12 (which has more refinements, as seen in the brochure). These models are all currently available to industry but a computerised version known as AB/12/COM is not currently available. We hope this will be ready at the time of the exhibition but we shall confirm a month prior to the show. Photographs showing machinery in situ are available.

Our network of dealers has been extended and we wish to stress the value of this to our industry. The products in themselves are not colourful and we would be happy to consider any proposal that will cause an immediate interest. We have other associated products – cutters, routers, spindles and spares – which all need to be displayed but in less prominent positions.

Our staff will wear their distinctive red blazers and grey trousers, or grey skirts for women. We envisage three separate sales stations, each self-contained with their own material and samples. A desk is needed for the receptionist, possibly positioned centre front. A rota board to indicate staff who are currently in attendance and an enclosed office and separate entertaining lounge are required.

*3. Definite requirements.* Machinery to have safety rails in accordance with Health and Safety requirements, to be provided on the three sales stations. An enclosed office with locking doors and three keys. Telephone and fax required. An entertainment area with space for three separate groupings with appropriate furniture, plus desk and chair for receptionist. Literature dispenser and cupboard space for brochures. Easy access for visitors to see products but restricted access to entertainment area. The stand to be well illuminated.

4. *Company particulars.* The company colours are red and black (colour references and logo style attached). Apart from these no other restrictions involved.

5. *Proposed budget.* For all standfitting contracting work inclusive of electrical installation and power consumption, floor coverings and furniture, plumbing, floral decor, photographs and captions and including dismantling and clearance at close to be 'on hire', we suggest a nominal budget allowance of £100 per square metre – excluding the design fee, which will accord to the scale of charges as stated in your professional association rate card, namely 10 per cent of the quoted contracting charge. The contractor's final invoices to be certified by you. Your fee will be apportioned according to these invoices. All machinery transport costs will be paid by us.

6. *Timetable.* Preliminary roughs to be available in three weeks, i.e. (date...). Final design required three weeks later, i.e. (date...). Specification and working drawings required four weeks later, i.e. (date...). Our final approval to be provided within three weeks of this time. Upon approval we require you to place this to tender with the four agreed stand builders. We expect to allow three weeks for estimates to be provided by the chosen contractors. We anticipate making our decision and placing the contract in approximately four months from today, i.e. (date...).

# CHOICE OF SITE

It is not always possible to choose the site at busy shows. Some organisers allocate sites according to their own judgement. Many exhibitions are categorised in product sections and the choice can be restricted. In long-established trade fairs, particularly overseas, regular exhibitors retain permanent pavilions. Some fairs have waiting lists and for the more popular events it is not unusual to wait two or three years before being allocated a site. As the years pass better sites become available and regular exhibitors can move up.

When it is possible to make a free choice a number of factors should be considered. All exhibitions have certain common characteristics such as main entrances, toilets, bars and refreshment areas, subsidiary entrances, car park exits and so on. All of these cause people movement. Views vary on what makes for a good stand position. However, the research that has been carried out on this subject suggests that when people enter an exhibition, a department store or similar situation, they will initially walk straight ahead, usually passing two intersecting gangways. The majority will then turn left or right rather than proceed straight ahead. Most men will turn left while the majority of women will turn right. Mixed couples will mostly turn right. This behaviour has been noticed in other public places where such a choice is available.

Some years ago a Canadian professor carried out tests in an effort to explain this behaviour but was unable to come up with an answer. It does, however, suggest that if yours is a male-oriented product, sites to the left of the central gangway could be more favourable and if it is a female-dominated product the reverse would be appropriate.

Stands adjoining bars and refreshment areas become cluttered with glasses and other rubbish and interested visitors get jostled. Staff on stands adjoining exits will see visitors leaving – often they are in a hurry and therefore not likely to be good sales prospects.

If it is possible to see a floor plan showing companies who have already booked space, try to be close to important companies or near to stands with any attractive activity. It is sometimes advantageous to be next to a strong competitor, particulary if it is considered that visitors could notice by comparison that yours is the superior product or that your prices are more competitive.

# STAND OPTIONS

Exhibitions normally offer the option of 'space only', where the exhibitor is responsible for all work and services, or 'shell scheme stands', where a section of the exhibition has been allocated into simple uniformly constructed stands. These are usually compact smaller units with walls, floor covering, nameboard and simple electrical work provided to an identical style. They are an economical method of participating at an exhibition. The stand-holder is normally permitted to add to the 'shell' and decorate at his own expense. Standfitters are adept at providing interesting interiors to these shell stands at reasonable prices. Many established exhibitors commenced exhibiting in this way.

Permanent stands can be manufactured to order in a modular format. They are made as demountable units permitting a variety of different combinations to be used. The usual module is 1 metre in width and 2 or 2.5 metres high. Obviously they are more expensive than 'on-hire' stands. However, with the increasing variations to the modular schemes that are becoming available, more of the regular exhibitors are taking this option and probably saving costs. Storage of such units is probably the biggest single item of cost, but if this can be done in the company's own premises, this problem does not arise.

*An interesting approach to the Philips stand at the NEC Motor Show, designed by Howard Hooper of IEDS. The product and company name are projected well. (Photograph courtesy of Philips and Post Studios Birmingham.)*

# 3

# CHOOSING THE DESIGNER

The designer's role is most important in contributing to the success of an exhibition project. Great care should be taken in selecting the best person for the event. Exhibition design is a specialised craft and should be carried out by a professional – not just anyone. The legendary story about the 'talented lady friend of the chairman's wife who is rather good at interior decoration' has been heard by all concerned in the exhibition business over the years: she is still completely useless at designing exhibition stands!

You will have prepared a full and considered brief reflecting the needs of the people and departments who are involved, and this should now be passed to a competent exhibition designer. There are several ways of making a choice if you do not know of an appropriate designer. For example, your advertising or PR agency can usually provide names of people or design organisations they have used with success for other clients. Some of the larger advertising agencies also have their own exhibition department. The Chartered Society of Designers maintain a register of their members and will provide names of designers qualified in the area that interests you (see Appendix 2).

Exhibition organisers will also be able to suggest people who have designed successful stands at their shows. For some industries, such as building and construction events, some architects will undertake exhibition design.

The final choice of designer depends on your requirements. If you decide on a 'shell scheme' at a minor exhibition, you will probably need only to establish a simple setting by means of display panels, self-standing display pieces, graphics and interesting arrangements of your own products. A good 'down-to-earth' designer can usually provide an adequate design at a realistic cost. Quite often the whole purpose of taking such a stand is to keep the cost down, often the case in a first-time exhibition. If you have booked 'space only', the whole stand has to be designed and built. This is your responsibility; the exhibition organisers only provide floor space.

The exhibition brief you have prepared will indicate the considered views of your company. It details the stand size and position, your general and particular requirements, a proposed budget and the timetable you wish to work to together with a list of exhibits and their requirements. You may have appointed the designer before you finalised the brief and budget, in which case the design contribution will already have been made and incorporated in the brief. If not, the full value of the written brief will now become apparent. Successful designers will have several projects happening at the same time and, like all creative people, they will appreciate the requirements and details being gathered together in a logical order so that they can devote their time and talent to creative rather than administrative work. Many designers charge on an hourly basis so if an agreed fee has not been negotiated, the time saved in having all details to hand is in fact your saving. It may have taken you some time to prepare the information that went into your brief but consider how much longer it would have taken the designer – a stranger to your company – to assimilate this information. Nevertheless, the designer will probably need to consult briefly with some of your staff who are involved or perhaps see the function of certain products before starting to design. This particularly applies to major trade shows with highly technical products.

# DESIGNERS' METHODS

Some designers are one- or two-people operations; others are part of a large practice. They will each have different methods of working. The designer who is part of a large practice will possibly have the services of a commercial person whose task it is to gather all the information, brochures and technical detail so that the designer – the creative interpreter – has everything to hand to allow him to create the exhibition stand. The commercial person will be the one who is in regular contact with the client – the exhibitor.

After the initial roughs are approved, the designer will usually prepare the final visual of the stand. Draughtsmen will prepare the working drawings and other details plus the specification, to the creative designer's instructions, when these are required. Upon approval of these, the commercial executive will tender the project to the chosen stand builders. These design teams can therefore work on several projects at once. For smaller stands it is not necessary to employ design groups but on a major international event or an Expo or other major trade fair, they often produce the better type of work. They are also likely to have greater knowledge of what is expected from exhibitors. On a project such as the Spanish Seville Expo, where the complete infrastructure has to be designed as well as the individual pavilions and display interior, architects and engineers are also often involved. These larger projects are tantamount to building a new town, the difference being that exhibition projects have to be built in a limited time and must be ready at the appointed hour. A smaller design establishment would not have the required experienced labour force.

Designers usually prefer to sketch out a few ideas or rough thoughts (known as 'scamps') and obtain the client's opinion before developing the final design. This will probably be in the form of a perspective drawing showing one or more frontages or sometimes the various elevations with a plan layout of the stand. Some exhibitors find it difficult to visualise plans and in such cases a simple model may be prepared. Models are an additional expense, warranted only if the client finds it necessary in the planning process for briefing the stand staff on the positions they will occupy within the stand, or maybe to explain the stand philosophy to senior management. They have little value to the designer or to the stand builders.

When the design presentation is approved by the client, working drawings and specifications are prepared. At this point the designer needs to obtain the organiser's and any other required approval. Working drawings and specifications are the most essential part of the design process. The drawings interpret design ideas in a realistic and practical manner which the building contractors can readily understand. Just as the client 'reads' the story of the stand from a model or visual, the craftsmen who are building it 'read' or visualise the final job from these drawings, which are fully described in the specification.

On a larger exhibition stand the designer will probably produce a plan, an elevation for each frontage, one or more sections plus details of any special features or displays. Accompanying these will be the specification, colour and finishes guide (sometimes shown on a drawing but preferably on a separate sheet), electrical layout and fittings (often overmarked on a drawing in colour together with a coded 'key' to provide a quick reference) plus details of any other special requirements needing separate layouts or drawings. These might include audio/video, compressed air, plumbing, floral decor, animation, hydraulics, etc. Smaller, less complex stands will require fewer drawings.

From all this information the exhibition standfitter will have all the facts that are needed to estimate the cost and he and his workmen will be able to build the stand just as the designer visualised it. At a later stage the standfitter will need signage and typographical information, preferably in layout or finished artwork form so that the art studio and signwriter can do their work. This may call for a specialised typographical design layout. Typographers will know the amount of space needed for any explanatory captions. If any captions are also to be in other languages – as will be the case at international or overseas events – the translations can increase the amount of space required. For example, from English into French the extra space needed could be 30 per cent and into Spanish and German maybe as much as 50 per cent.

## STANDFITTERS' DESIGNERS

Some standfitters and contractors have their own design departments capable of producing adequate simple designs. Many of those who manufacture modular schemes have a wide choice of component parts available. Often they use computer-generated design to develop their ideas: such techniques are becoming popular and will be used increasingly in the future. They are quick and can be cost-effective both to the client and contractor. One criticism, however, is that such designs have a certain 'sameness' about them, much as Lego-built toys have. This problem will be overcome as users become more skilful in their use of computer-assisted design systems.

Salesmen from some modular component manufacturing companies maintain that their systems make a positive contribution to the environment since they are not wasteful in any way. They are manufactured from strong aluminium supports into which are fitted strong high-density particle-board panels. They have a long life and when they become worn they are recycled and re-start their display use, with virtually no waste. Many component pieces are already available and, as an indication of their success, some stands constructed using these systems have won design awards for originality.

## TENDERING

The designer is usually asked to tender the standfitting work after the design and working drawings have been approved by the client. His standfitter recommendations are usually sought by the exhibitor. Because he has frequent dealings with these standfitters they are unlikely to upset a regular client.

Whilst tendering is the norm for official organisations and larger companies, many smaller exhibitors find it better to negotiate a contract. Negotiated contracts usually come about after a relationship has been established over a period of time between a standfitter and his client. The contractor will have shown that he is fair in his dealings and costings and can be relied upon to complete the work on time. Experienced exhibition managers who are themselves capable of estimating a project at current prices often use this method.

When considering estimates the old rule always applies – 'You always get what you pay for'! Regrettably there are instances where standfitters will take a chance and cut their prices to obtain immediate work, especially if they are 'light' in a particular show. Their subsequent workmanship could well show their 'saving'. In the worst-case scenario they can (and do) go broke just as the work is due to be started on site – not the best time to search for another standfitter at a busy show.

The main standfitting contractor will normally be able to cope with all aspects of the work that the designer has called for within the design. As a general example this will include floor coverings, furniture, plumbing, electrical or gas services, floral displays, compressed air, audio/video, television and satellite signal distribution, computer 'clean lines' and any other services.

Telephone, telex and fax services usually have to be specifically ordered by the stand holder. The telephone companies will only deal directly with the end user. The designer, however, will normally specify the position of the instruments on the stand.

Stand cleaning is sometimes provided by the show organisers within the space rental and sometimes by specified contractors. Sometimes exhibitors may be required to make their own arrangements.

For some projects the designer may suggest that certain supplementary services should be bought in as separate entities. This could save the 10 or 15 per cent handling charge that the main contractor would normally add on the 'bought-in services'.

The whole of the stand and all services included will be quoted as being provided 'on hire' for the duration of the exhibition unless different arrangements have been made. An 'outright sale stand' may cost more. (The reader may like to know how this 'on-hire' arrangement originated. It dates back to the times after the Second World War when timber was in short supply and could only be obtained with a licence. By the 'on-hire' method, stand-builders were able to save the stands and build up their stocks. The system still remains.)

Because photoprints and captions are specially mounted onto individual panels for exhibitors' specific needs, standfitters will usually agree to an exhibitor taking them away at the conclusion of the exhibition at no extra charge. Electrical fittings, flower troughs and plants, telephones and similar items are 'on hire' and will be collected by their owners after the exhibition closes. (The 'on-hire' philosophy here is that if these items were charged at the correct purchase price, the stand cost would be greater than that quoted.) If the exhibitor removes them a charge could be made by the owner.

## TIMESCALE

Once the project passes to the designer a strict timescale must be observed. This has already been indicated in the design brief detailed in the last chapter. The designer now has your proposals and he will confirm his acceptance of these together with the agreed timetable. While a little leeway will not prove greatly harmful, longer delays could.

In preparing the brief the exhibition manager will have noted all his requirements and in doing so a tentative critical path and timescale will have been created. This must now be completed. Since every case is different it is only possible to indicate how it might read. For example, we now know the time the designer needs for each stage, usually 3-4 weeks. The standfitter needs 2-3 weeks to prepare an estimate. They prefer to have a firm decision on future work that has to be produced, say 6-8 months in advance of the exhibition opening day if this can be achieved. This allows time to plan their works programme and buy in any special items that may be required for the project.

With this information a firm timescale and operational plan can be produced and circulated to the departments concerned. In an ideal situation this would now read:

Designer briefed . . . . . . . . . . . . . . . . . . . . . . . . .4/1/95
Preliminary roughs submitted . . . . . . . . . . . . .24/1/95
Prelim: roughs agreed . . . . . . . . . . . . . . . . . . .1/2/95
Final design submitted . . . . . . . . . . . . . . . . . .21/2/95
Final design agreed . . . . . . . . . . . . . . . . . . . .25/2/95
Working drawings and specification submitted .18/3/95
Working drawings approved . . . . . . . . . . . . . .22/3/95
Submitted to tender . . . . . . . . . . . . . . . . . . . .23/3/95
Tenders received . . . . . . . . . . . . . . . . . . . . . . .4/4/95
Standfitting contract placed . . . . . . . . . . . . . .6/4/95
Total time span for design . . . . . . . . . . . . . .13 weeks

The above indicates a typical timespan which then allows the stand builder six months in which to prepare the stand before moving onto the site to commence building. He will probably have 7-10 days to build, receive exhibits and hand over to the exhibitor.

## STAFF EARLY WARNING

As we consider the timescale other factors inevitably arise. The transport manager needs to know in good time the demands that will be placed on his department. If special vehicles are required he may need to hire them specifically. The works manager will need as much notification as possible regarding any products needing special preparation.

Staff requirements should be assessed and the people involved should be warned in adequate time. Holidays, weddings, overseas visits and many other situations so easily sabotage the best perceived plan. Some exhibition staff may also need to attend training courses, seminars and workshops. Now is the time to consider these aspects, whilst there is still time in hand. It is also wise to establish which of your sales staff have experience of working at an exhibition or trade show. It is not the same as being on the road!

It may also prove useful to arrange in-house seminars. These can be beneficial, particularly if adequate time is allowed for question and answer sessions. All these requirements will be dealt with in depth in the appropriate chapters in this book. In so many cases simple problems seem to arise rather too late in the run-up to the exhibition, causing complications that could so easily have been avoided with forethought.

*Boat Show Stand at Earls Court 2 in 1991 illustrating vividly the good access to exhibits, tidiness and excellent lighting both at the Stand and in the Hall. (Photograph provided by Earls Court, photography by QFT)*

# 4

# CHOOSING THE STANDFITTING CONTRACTOR

Having completed the design, working drawings and specification in accordance with the agreed timescale and obtained approval, the designer will submit the project to tender to an agreed number of standfitting contractors. The designer will choose those contractors he considers to be equal in ability and capable of building the project. It is no use asking two different types of contractors to quote against each other: everyone recognises the difference between a Rolls Royce and a Ford – the same analogy applies to standfitters.

Normally the tenders are requested for a definite date when they will all be opened together. It is common for the company secretary to be present with the EM and designer to ensure absolute impartiality. For our example of 450 square metres let us assume that four standfitters have provided estimates as follows:

*Company* . . . . . . . . . . . . . . . . . . . . . . . . . . . . . . .*Quotation*

| | |
|---|---|
| 1. AB Exhibition Company. | £38,700 |
| 2. Smith & Jones Exhibitions | £46,350 |
| 3. Worldwide Construction Ltd | £44,100 |
| 4. Brown Brothers Ltd | £45,225 |
| Total | £174,375 |

The average of these is therefore £43,593, or £96.87 per square metre.

Assuming all four are considered to be equal in ability and reliability, two possible methods of choosing the successful builder can be considered: either accept the lowest quotation or choose the nearest price to the average. It is notable that the first on the list is considerably lower than the others. What is the reason for this? Is this standfitter short of work or has he made a mistake? It would be worthwhile finding out. The answer may influence your decision. Having resolved this, the budget can be prepared and contracts placed. The designer's fee can also be established. (In Chapter 2, this was nominated as 10 per cent of the standfitting contractor's contract price.)

## PLANNING THE BUDGET

Earlier, when the decision to exhibit was taken, an initial figure was discussed. Now that a clearer picture has been established, a properly conceived budget needs to be prepared. This should show all aspects such as cost of space, design fee, standfitting work, including all incidental items, publicity and PR together with any other bought-in items.

Internal and staff expenses, including hotels, travelling costs and exhibit transport, can all be considered as internal costs. It will not be possible to establish accurately all of these costs at this stage, in which case an approximation should be made. At some trade fairs, particularly overseas, it is necessary to enter a ballot for space, in which case the final cost will not be known until the ballot has taken place. Since these ballots conform to a system of size groups, the differences in costs will not be great. For example, the group for which you have applied might be the 400-425 square metres group. Your stand could be any size within these parameters, but the difference in cost – for example, between 425 and 450 square metres – is not going to affect you greatly.

It should be remembered that certain items will often exceed the budget allocations. A typical example is artwork: photography, transparencies, typographical layouts and typesetting nearly always cost more than the allowance made. They are often specified late and it becomes necessary to employ labour on overtime in the display studios. This can double or treble the expected cost. When asked to quote a cost the suppliers will estimate on the safe side and quote a PC sum (prime cost sum). This is the sum they have estimated, but in the final invoicing they will specify what they have actually supplied and charge this figure plus their overheads and profit mark-up. This may have little similarity to the quoted PC sum. Always beware of PC items. If they can be avoided, it is wise to do so.

## BUDGET HEADINGS

Most exhibitions and trade fairs contain very similar ingredients. It is possible, therefore, to devise a budget structure which should meet the needs of most exhibitors, whether at trade fairs or public events. The costs will always be either 'bought in' or 'internal'. The headings in our sample format will provide a basis that can be used to meet most situations that will arise. However, because all exhibitions and trade fairs are different it is not possible to be totally accurate in allocating headings.

It is recommended that the budget column should be completed at the outset and the actual figures inserted as soon as they are known. This will establish a tight budget control. Contingencies should always be included. In our example 5-7.5 per cent is used. This must be left to the discretion of the exhibition manager.

BOUGHT-IN ITEMS

| 1. Organiser's charges | Budgeted cost | Actual cost |
|---|---|---|
| Exhibition space | ................... | ................ |
| Shell scheme stand | ................... | ................ |
| Tickets, passes and staff badges | ................... | ................ |
| Exhibition catalogue advertisement | ................... | ................ |

*2. Specialist charges*
Exhibition stand designer ....................... ...................
Typographer ....................... ...................
Animation designer ....................... ...................

*3. Stand contracting charges*
Standfitting ....................... ...................
Electrical ....................... ...................
Plumbing ....................... ...................
Furniture and floorcovering ....................... ...................
Telephone, fax and telex ....................... ...................
Floral decoration ....................... ...................
Typesetting, captions and signage ....................... ...................
Photographs and transparencies ....................... ...................
Stand cleaning ....................... ...................
Exhibit transportation ....................... ...................
Machinery lifting and cranage ....................... ...................

*4. Publicity and promotion*
Newspaper advertising ....................... ...................
Trade journal advertising ....................... ...................
Design and production ....................... ...................
Brochures and leaflets ....................... ...................
PR staff and expenses ....................... ...................
Photography ....................... ...................
Special promotions ....................... ...................
Entertaining ....................... ...................

INTERNAL AND STAFF

Exhibition preparation ....................... ...................
Transport ....................... ...................
Staff uniforms or dresses ....................... ...................
Staff subsistence ....................... ...................
Hotels ....................... ...................
Temporary staff ....................... ...................
Training films and seminars ....................... ...................
Travel allowance ....................... ...................

Provisional total .......................

Contingency @ .... per cent .......................

Estimated/actual total ....................... ...................

# A SAMPLE BUDGET

Using the format indicated we can now complete the budget, using the information that has been established. This will provide a budget cost.

EXHIBITION: Advanced Woodworking Machinery Trade Show
DATE: 12-17 October 1995
VENUE: The Exhibition Centre, London
STAND NUMBER: 5/512. Two sides open. Size 25 x 18m = 450m²

Build-up commences 3 October 1995. Break-up 18-21 October 1995
Date Budget Prepared 5 April 1995 by Exhibition Manager H. Smith.

BOUGHT-IN ITEMS

| | Budgeted cost | Actual cost |
|---|---|---|
| *1. Organiser's charges* | | |
| Exhibition space @ £85 per m² | £38,250 | |
| Shell scheme | N/A | |
| Tickets passes and staff badges (allowance) | £150 | |
| Catalogue advertisement 1 page | £250 | |
| | | |
| *Specialist charges* | | |
| Stand designer (10% of average charges) | £4359 | |
| Typographer | (included in above) | |
| Animation designer | N/A | |
| | | |
| *Stand contracting charges* | | |
| Standfitting | £38,700 | |
| Electrical | (included in above) | |
| Plumbing | N/A | |
| Furniture and flooring | (included in above) | |
| Telephone and fax | (estimated at £350) | |
| Floral decoration | (estimated at £175) | |
| Typeset: captions and signs | (PC allowance £600) | |
| Photographs and trans. | (PC allowance £500) | |
| Stand cleaning | (included in space cost) | |
| Exhibit transport | (estimated at £1200) | |
| Machinery lifting on site | (PC allowance £800) | |
| | | |
| *Publicity and promotion* | | |
| Newspaper advertising | N/A | |

Trade journal advertising     (PC allowance £1750)
Design and production     (PC allowance £1000)
Brochures and leaflets     (PC allowance £2000)
PR staff and expenses:     (allowance of £1500
    from yearly fee)
Photography     (PC allowance £200)
Special promotions     nil
Entertaining     (from sales budget)

INTERNAL AND STAFF COSTS

Exhibit preparation (in-house labour allowance) £2000
Transportation (staff cars and rail fares)     £850
Staff uniforms/dresses (reusable)     £1840
Staff subsistence (12 @ £80 x 10 days)     £9600
Hotels (allowance included in subsistence)     N/A
Temporary staff (one person estimated)     £300
Training films (hire charge)     £100
Travel allowance (12 @ £20)     £240

Provisional total     £105,214

Contingency @ 7.5% per cent     £7,891

Estimated total     £113,105

Based upon the information we have available, this is a logical estimate of cost. From the beginning we had estimated design costs reasonably accurately. The stand building cost came in at a lower level than was originally estimated but when all other costs are also included such as publicity and promotion, transport of exhibits, staff costs, etc., the figure may seem high. The value of individually specifying all items is now clearly seen. So often, companies attend exhibitions and trade fairs without clearly knowing or even understanding what is involved in their total cost. Many forget to include their own additional internal costs. If economies or alterations need to be made, now is the time to revise the thinking or the size of stand.

At first sight, it would appear that a large number of estimated, or PC, items are included in the sample budget. It is worth considering why this has come about. Typesetting, captions, photographs and transparencies will be required, but at this time details have not been discussed or finalised. Similarly, it is planned to take machines to the exhibition but until the EM has sufficient information it is not possible to obtain a quotation from the specialist machinery movers.

The advertising schedule will be planned by the publicity manager when sufficient information is available. When this time arrives it will be possible to provide an accurate cost of advertising in the trade journals, preparing the design and production of the advertisements and brochures and deciding what new photographs are required. Until then we have to make inspired guesses based upon earlier experiences. It is no use completely leaving these costs – which amount to almost £5000 – out of the budget calculations, since this would not be helpful to anyone.

## PLACING THE CONTRACT

The standfitting contractors need to know your decision as early as possible. They will be quoting for other work and need to balance their quota for various exhibition and fairs. If a designer has undertaken the work, he will have provided the specification and tender documentation. He will also reply to those tendering. It is quite usual that standfitters are informed of other prices in a letter of rejection, but not who provided each price. The rejection would then probably read as follows:

Thank you for submitting your quotation, based upon our specification and drawings, in respect of exhibition stand at the Advanced Woodworking Machinery Trade Show being held on 12-17 October, 1995, at The Exhibition Centre, London. Our clients have instructed us to accept another quotation.

For your information, the tenders received for this work were as follows: £38,700, £44,100, £45,225, £46,350.

Thank you for your speedy cooperation. We hope to ask you to provide estimates for other work in the future.

The acceptance letter will read:

Thank you for your quotation of (date) which our clients have instructed us to accept. The client's official purchase order will follow in the next two or three days.

The designer responsible for this work will be Mr Arthur Brown, who will be sending you three further sets of drawings. The client's exhibition manager is Mr Harry Smith, whom you will meet in due course. As in all of our work, no alteration to specification is permitted unless authorised by our designer in charge.

We look forward to working with you to the successful completion of this project.

All the required information is contained in these letters. If the exhibitor has requested the tender himself, they can be adapted appropriately.

Within his fee structure, the designer is then expected to progress the work through all stages to completion on site and keep the EM informed through regular progress meetings.

Some standfitters will ask for a deposit. This is a subject for negotiation. If a designer or consultant is employed, they can advise. If the exhibitor is dealing direct, a negotiated answer can usually be found.

## SUBCONTRACTORS

If subcontractors are to be employed, their contracts or methods of working should be arranged at this time. The designer – if one is employed – should be kept informed at all stages since it is his duty to incorporate all such work within the scheme.

Telephones, fax or telex should also be ordered at this time. Again the designer will need to indicate positions of apparatus. If the exhibition is a public or consumer type event, security would also need to be considered and a cost allocated.

# INSURANCE

Both the exhibition stand and all of its parts – that is, the construction, hired items such as furniture and floor coverings, electrical and any other parts – must all be insured against third-party risks, damage and theft. Since the goods are provided to you on hire, you become liable for all of these risks at all times the stand is on site, even when you are not there.

Stand personnel also must be insured against all the usual risks. In the case of overseas exhibitions – for example, in the Middle East – what would be simple personal risks in the UK could become major risks.

Most insurance companies will extend company insurance to cover an exhibition all-parties risk for a reasonable premium. In the case of other risks, the exhibition organiser will normally arrange for realistic insurance cover to be available, via specialist brokers, usually at Lloyd's.

Insurance should be arranged directly the standfitting contract is placed. Losses do happen at exhibitions and trade fairs, usually during the build-up and dismantling periods – the most dangerous loss periods. Some exhibits also need to be insured through the transportation period. If frozen foods and foodstuffs are being transported to site in refrigerated trucks and then to a freezer cabinet on the stand, there will be a vulnerable period.

Insurance naturally leads to considerations of security; this will be considered in a later chapter.

# INTERNAL REQUIREMENTS

The most important part of any exhibition or trade fair are the exhibits – the whole reason for being there! Many firms spend a great deal of money on preparing their exhibits so that they are seen in the best possible light. It is not good practice to take just any exhibit off the store-room racks and send it down to the stand; you do want to impress the prospective buyer.

The works manager should by now be very involved in the forthcoming event. He should know the classification of the products he is expected to provide and when they are required on site. He should be given a budget sum for product preparation. If an operative is required to demonstrate a machine or piece of equipment, that should also be discussed at this time. If the occasion is a public event then special offers, demonstrators, uniforms and dresses will be needed. All these items should be discussed in detail. (Overseas show requirements will be discussed later in a separate chapter.)

Many companies do not allocate a job number to their internal work and often do not get down to the details until quite late in the day. This planning is a very important part of event preparation and should be treated as such and not as a nuisance, as many departments do.

At this time it is useful also to discuss transport needs with the appropriate manager. He may have to hire special low-loader vehicles if you have large machinery, or refrigerated vans or some other type of vehicle. He would certainly need to know the time-scale involved well in advance.

# 5

# LOGISTICS

At the time you sign the application for space you agree to observe the exhibition organiser's rules and regulations, a copy of which should have been provided before you signed the contract, agreement or application for space. This is always a condition of entry into any exhibition or trade fair in the UK or overseas. These rules and regulations incorporate those conditions imposed upon the exhibition or trade fair organiser by the hall or venue owner. They also incorporate any statutory requirements imposed on both hall owner and organiser by the county authority, building inspectors, fire authorities, venue insurers and the Health and Safety Executive. All those involved agree to notify and ensure that the next person in the line will follow the necessary requirements. This is why exhibition contracts and agreements are generally so long with so much small print.

Although they are not the most interesting documents, they should be read carefully by the exhibition manager and anyone else concerned with building or providing exhibits or machinery. They do make good sense and if all exhibitors followed them and the dates and conditions stated, it would make the organisers' job much easier.

# EXHIBITORS' MANUALS

Exhibitors are provided with a book of instructions and forms when they are allocated their space. This is referred to as the exhibitors' manual, exhibition book or some similar title. It should contain all the information that an exhibitor is likely to need to build the stand. All organisers have their own ideas of what is needed, and the manual should carry an index of all their requirements and services, which typically would include the following:

| | |
|---|---|
| Access plan to venue | Logo format |
| Accommodation details | Lorry passes |
| Advertisements | Machinery lifting |
| Badges and passes | Maintenance |
| Banking facilities | Nameboards |
| Build-up and breakdown dates | Opening hours |
| Car parking | Organiser's contact names |
| Catering on stands | Organiser's forms |
| Checklist | Patents Act |
| Cloakrooms | Photographers |
| Contractors, list of | Photographs |
| Demonstrators and temps | Post offices |
| Description of exhibits | Poster sites |
| Electrical contractors | Press and visitor promotion |
| Exhibition catalogue | Press office |
| Exhibitors' badges | Press packs |
| Exhibitors' invitations | Press previews |
| Exhibits – delivery and handling | Private rooms and suites |
| Fire precautions | Product category index |
| First aid facilities | Promotional material |
| Florists | Registered Design Act |
| Food hygiene regulations | Restaurants |
| Forwarding/shipping agents | Sales training films |
| Furniture and floor covering hire | Security |
| Gas | Shell scheme contractors |
| General services and information | Shell scheme specification |
| HM Customs and Excise | Sponsors |
| Health and Safety at Work Act | Stand cleaning |
| Insurance | Stand plan submission |
| Interpreters | Storage |

| | |
|---|---|
| Technical services | Video advertising |
| Telephones | Visitor and buyer promotion |
| Toilets | Water and waste services |
| Trade Descriptions Act | Workmen's passes |

All of these items have to be detailed in the manual. In the case of various Acts and Laws an extract of the appropriate part is sufficient; other items should carry an explanation under a subsequent entry in the book. The index should provide the relevant page numbers. Items relating to the Press, visitor promotion and other similar headings should be dealt with in detail in their own particular section of the manual.

Manuals can often contain as many as a hundred pages or more on a large trade fair. Some exhibition managers find it convenient to photocopy the particular pages applying to a department – for example, the PR and publicity department – and let them deal with the entry, but always via the EM so that he or she can tick the item off on the progress schedule. The page number of each of the headings should be noted since many pages will be duplicated or triplicated and have to be returned to the appropriate person, supplier or department within the exhibition organisation for action. On all of these pages a latest return date is usually indicated, which should be honoured.

Exhibitions and trade fairs will carry different headings to accommodate the requirements of the industry which is being displayed. Those shown above are merely indicative of a typical event but are among the most common.

Quite often an organiser will permit suppliers to advertise in the manual. This is a very good medium for the supplier since every person reading it is an exhibitor or involved in some way and therefore a likely prospect. There is little wastage. For the organiser the income from the advertisers can pay for the cost of the manual.

# FORM FILLING

The various forms relating to the subject matter of the exhibition need to be completed and sent to the organiser. Most people dislike filling in forms. Because of this, the EM will find it difficult to gather the information needed – everyone puts it off until tomorrow. The organisers have to have this information to open the exhibition or fair successfully on time. Most have a progress department whose task is to ensure the required information is received. Some organisers are now introducing penalties for the late arrival of forms; some don't even bother to chase the information at all. The latter is sometimes the case with overseas trade fairs, so that when the exhibitor arrives on site and discovers he has no lighting, floor covering or furniture he has to manage as well as he can! If he succeeds in persuading a supplier to provide the required item, the cost could be quite enormous and he may get the left-overs. Organisers are often arranging three or four trade fairs at the same time, involving perhaps two or three thousand exhibitors, so they cannot really be blamed for the inefficiency of an overseas exhibitor or be expected to chase around for him.

Many trade fair and exhibition organisers request exhibitors to submit a drawing of the stand for their approval. This is in order to ensure the stand will meet the requirements of the various authorities. Organisers do not want exhibition stands condemned at the last moment by a building inspector. If a double-deck stand is being used, for example, the constructional drawings may have to be approved by the local authority building inspectors and surveyors and, in some areas, also by the fire department. Regulations vary and a form and appropriate explanation will be supplied in the exhibition manual.

If a shell scheme is being used, nameboard details will be required. When a choice of items such as furniture and display units are allowed and included within the shell-scheme, these also have to be detailed on the appropriate form.

# INVOLVING AND BRIEFING OTHER DEPARTMENTS

To obtain the information needed to complete the forms in the manual, enquiries will have to be made of other people in the company. This is a good time for the EM to comprehensively brief the others who are concerned. If the EM has circulated details of the exhibition or trade fair to all departments at an earlier time, he can now fill in all incidental details. He will need a list of the personnel attending and when they will be attending to ensure they have exhibition passes and car parking stickers. Their accommodation requirements also have to be established. Any special requirements stipulated by the organiser – for example, on electrical needs and other energy sources – can be discussed and, where necessary, the appropriate person can be put in direct contact with the designer. It is, however, likely that the designer will already have foreseen the need to speak with the various specialists and asked the EM to arrange a meeting.

Sometimes it is useful to photocopy parts of the manual to give to others involved in the stand. The organiser will rarely issue a second copy of the manual because this could cause duplication of an instruction. On a large project this could prove costly.

# BADGES, TICKETS AND PASSES

Having collected all the information on requirements, the EM can complete the form requesting passes and badges. He must ensure that sufficient passes are ordered. They are normally included in the exhibition space charges so there is no excuse for shortages. The company's directors do become rather cross when, having decided to see how the stand building is progressing, they find they cannot gain access to the venue because they had no pass. It does happen frequently! (Visitors' tickets will be dealt with in a later chapter under promotion.)

# PROVIDING PRELIMINARY INFORMATION TO OVERSEAS AGENTS

Since overseas personnel have to make travelling and other arrangements, it is helpful to provide them with early advance information. Trade fair dates and times are probably all they require at this time. This will at least remind them to notify staff and clients who they may wish to attend.

## SURVEYING THE EXHIBITION VENUE

The EM should survey the venue and surrounding district early in the run-up period. A decent hotel will be required for those who are away from home. If it is an entirely strange location, it is useful to spend a couple of nights at the chosen hotel to ascertain the level of the facilities. Some hotels offer a sports centre within the complex, which may be appreciated by staff who have been working all day in the dry atmosphere of an exhibition hall. Swimming pool or squash court facilities can also be most welcome. The EM should also explore the restaurants and cafes on offer. Any other nightspots might also prove attractive to VIP visitors.

By the time the EM has spent a couple of days in the area, visited the venue press department and the hotel and hospitality department that are present at the larger centres, he should have a reasonable idea of the facilities on offer. This information can be incorporated into an information book that may be issued to staff who are to work at the exhibition. The EM should also meet all the departmental heads, managers and foremen with whom he will be working at the time of the exhibition.

## NOTIFYING STAFF REQUIREMENTS

By this time, all departments will have details about the exhibition. Managers will have notified the EM of their ticket and staff accommodation requirements and other such logistical arrangements. Now is the time to ensure that the chosen staff know they are required to be at the exhibition or trade fair on certain dates in the future. It is amazing how many people will come up with reasons why they cannot be available when they are required. Holidays and weddings always seem to intervene at exhibition times! This problem must be overcome by the departmental heads.

Having allocated staff, bookings must be made at the chosen hotel. This is not always easy since at exhibition times many regular exhibitors will have booked their hotel accommodation the previous year before they vacated.

## STAFF SEMINARS

Working at an exhibition is entirely different from being on the road. Sales staff and any others who are to work on the exhibition stand either selling or demonstrating a product must be trained properly. Many films now exist for this purpose, and they can be hired at a reasonable daily or weekly cost. It is advantageous for the sales manager to arrange one or more sales seminars for those who are to be working at the exhibition. If he or she does not have the experience to undertake this task, freelance seminar leaders can be brought in. Many exhibition and trade fair organisers arrange exhibition sales seminars, often in conveniently located centres, such as London, Birmingham, Manchester and Glasgow, which enables exhibitors from most regions of the UK to attend.

## STAFF UNIFORMS

If it is decided to use a special uniform or dress now is the time to establish the requirements and order as necessary. A simple uniform style could, for example, be red blazers and grey trousers for men and red blazers and grey skirts or slacks for women. Many variations of this theme can be devised with a little thought. Uniform dress does distinguish the staff and is therefore helpful to visitors.

Name badges should always be worn, identical in style and in an identical position on the lapel. The visitor can then identify whom he is speaking to.

## STAND CATERING

Catering can be estimated and decided later. On a busy show, particularly public events, airline type tray meals can be provided for staff; if this is done, a private staffroom must be incorporated in the stand design. If it is intended to offer snack meals to visitors, the necessary requirements must be calculated and specimen menus considered.

## SCHEDULING AND PROGRESSING

We have now reached the stage where we have arranged the design, ordered the stand-building and become familiar with the needs shown in the exhibition manual. Many events leading up to the exhibition or trade fair are now happening and as the weeks pass by even more will need to be incorporated into our plans. The progress schedule provides the indication when the next item needs to be actioned. This schedule is in fact an extension of the work already done. The design brief established the requirements we decided were necessary, the drawings which resulted were tendered and a standfitting contractor appointed and the budget created.

We now have to continue that work and establish a list of action dates to ensure that the correct event happens when it should. This could be called a critical path, progress schedule or any other title that appeals. Its purpose is to indicate the requirement, the planned date and the actual date the item is achieved. The headings here are similar to those we used earlier on in the budget.

| ITEM | TARGET DATE | DATE ACHIEVED |
|---|---|---|
| *Stand building requirements* | | |
| Order stand-fitting | 6 April 1995 | 7 April 1995 |
| Order electrics | ditto | ditto |
| Order floor covering | ditto | ditto |
| Order furniture | ditto | ditto |
| Order telephone services | 18 April | |
| Order stand cleaning | 18 April | |
| | | |
| *On site* | | |
| Book hotel accommodation | 26 April | |
| Order catering requirements | 30 April | |
| | | |
| *Organiser's requirements* (subdivide as necessary) | | |
| Car park passes | 19 July | |
| Staff badges | 12 Sept | |
| Maintenance passes | ditto | |
| Workmen's passes | ditto | |
| Lorry passes | ditto | |
| Catalogue entry | 8 August | |
| Catalogue advertisement | ditto | |
| Visitor invitation tickets | 1 August | |
| Publicity packs | 8 August | |
| | | |
| *Publicity PR and promotion* (subdivide as necessary) | | |
| Arrange new photographs | 1 June | |
| Write captions for exhibits | 31 August | |
| Order leaflets | 31 August | |
| Order brochure15 August | 15 August | |
| Arrange stand photographer | 5 September | |
| Security | 5 September | |
| Arrange transport needs | 17 August | |
| Staff training films | 31 August | |
| Staff seminars | 31 August | |
| Arrange staff stand rota | 31 August | |
| Order staff uniforms | 17 August | |
| Commence stand-building | 3 October | |
| Exhibition manager move to site | 4 October | |
| First consignment of exhibits to site | 7 October | |
| Staff briefing on site | 11 October | |

| | |
|---|---|
| Press day | 12 October |
| Closing day | 17 October |
| Clear exhibits (commence) | 18 October |
| Vacate stand and check for damage | 21 October |
| Prepare exhibition report | 2 November |
| Inquest | 16 November |

This schedule indicates the nature of information that might be expected. The target date should always be realistic and the aim must be to achieve it. However, a few days either way will not usually seriously upset the schedule though it is sensible to endeavour to meet set dates – otherwise why have them? The schedule should be updated daily on the run-up to the event.

# 6

# PUBLICITY, PROMOTION AND PR

All exhibitors seek publicity for their products – that is one of the reasons they are attending an exhibition or trade fair: to gain publicity and exposure. The more competitive the product, the greater the publicity effort needed. This is why the more popular public events such as Homes and Gardens, DIY, TV and Radio Shows are advertised so heavily when they are imminent on posters, newspapers, radio and TV and other popular media outlets.

Trade fairs need maximum exposure to their audience in the particular industry to which they are appealing and normally use trade journals together with quality daily and weekly newspapers, particularly those which publish supplements or features. The financial press and the Sunday quality papers are also used. Radio and television programmes such as Tomorrow's World and similar series are good vehicles if they are transmitted immediately before the exhibition, but only a limited number of the listeners or viewers – those with an interest in that industry – will actually attend the exhibition.

Direct mail plays a large part in trade and industrial fairs but not nearly as much in public events. If, however, tickets are being sent to selected retailers to distribute to their special customers in order for them to visit a popular public event, direct mail can be of value.

If the trade fair is planned to be 'International', the foreign media should also be informed and then very much earlier planning becomes necessary. This is why overseas agents need to be notified early so they may make their arrangements. Your export sales staff should be given advance notice so that they can commence discussions with their customers early in the day.

It is helpful to airline carriers if they are given advance notification of a fair, particularly if it is likely that additional flights may be needed for the exhibition period. Airlines themselves frequently publicise the event – they also are looking for extra business. Firms that are frequent exhibitors will have their own specialist department to prepare their advance publicity and promotional material – usually the publicity department or their advertising agent or sometimes a specialist exhibition promotion and/or PR agency. No matter which, they will all follow a similar path. PR is the starting point for all companies exhibiting. The very fact that the company is exhibiting means that they have something they want to show or say! It may be a new range of products, opening a new factory, going into new market areas – all of these are reason enough for publicising.

Trade journals fill their pages with stories such as these as a matter of course, so this is where the exhibition PR starts. In the months building up to the exhibition the initial stories can be developed and extended. Foreign versions should be sent to overseas agents for publication in their trade journals (always written in the language of that country). Where available, photographs with a brief caption should also be included. Sometimes they are published; it's always worth trying.

If you do not have very much to say about your product it is often possible to write an interesting story about the personalities involved or working in your company or schemes that you have introduced that benefit customers or maybe the environment. Most companies that are exhibiting have something interesting to say – it's a question of analysing the purpose of your participation – hence the growth of the professional PR agencies specialising in this type of work. Public events can also benefit from similar treatment but the PR stories do not have to start so early. The popular press and magazines tend to seek stories that highlight people rather than products, but any good human appeal story is likely to attract the editor's attention – particularly if there is a shortage of news items for that day or issue.

With radio and TV it is essential to 'sell' the producer a good idea that could attract listeners or viewers. They will not consider an approach that is too blatantly commercial, but if it has novelty appeal it will stand a chance.

## ADVERTISEMENTS

Most trade journals have at least one special issue devoted to the trade fair and usually publish a floor plan with a list of exhibitors and a summary of products. Reviewers provide opinions on products and services and evaluate industry developments. Such issues usually carry a 'bumper' crop of advertisements for the companies who are exhibiting, all including 'See our stand No. XXX.' Special issues have become a ritual at most trade fairs and exhibitors do seem to support them. Usually only one or two major publications will attract the majority of exhibitors and buyers, so choose wisely. The national and international press should also be considered if the fair is a large major event.

Whatever advertising is employed attention must always be drawn to the stand number, hall and any other quick identifying landmark – such as 'facing the entrance', 'near to the Toby Bar', etc. These may seem minor details but it is essential to take every opportunity to remind readers that you are waiting to give them every attention – on your stand! Any invitation tickets or letters that are sent should mention the stand number and hall and the easiest way to find it; letter stickers are often provided by the organiser for this purpose. A plan on the back of the invitation ticket showing your stand is helpful. The timing of the advertisement is important. If the paper is publishing a special supplement obviously this is the time to appear.

The financial press is also important – more so to some companies than others, but the exhibitor who always advertised in the financial press 'because the Chairman expected to read exhibition reviews there rather than in other papers' is advertising for the wrong reason. There is, of course, nothing wrong with advertising in the financial press – particularly if the product or service is likely to

*Phineas T. Barnham presented 'The Greatest Show on Earth' at Olympia in 1888-89, thus starting the traditional Christmas Show. The last Bertram Mills show was in 1967. (Photograph courtesy of Olympia/Earls Court.)*

appeal to that readership – but there must be a more valid promotional reason than a Chairman's whim! If the exhibiting company is also enjoying a good PR story in the same issue this could be a good reason for advertising.

With the major public events, the consumer press, newspapers and popular magazines (not forgetting some children's and teenage publications, depending on the subject) will be filling their pages with advertisements relating to the exhibition. All of these must be considered; they might be carrying stories praising the value of your particular product.

The exhibition will have its own catalogue in which all exhibitors will be included with an entry describing their exhibit. This is usually restricted to a stated number of words, but it is usually also possible to advertise in this. Many visitors to trade fairs retain the catalogue as a product guide for use in their work at a later stage, and this should be borne in mind when advertising in it.

Overseas trade journals often review major British trade fairs so it can be worth considering advertising in the leading trade journals of countries that are of interest to you. Your local agent should be able to assist with this.

## INVITATION TICKETS – MAILING LIST

Exhibition organisers make tickets available for exhibitors to send to their customers. If these are correctly used they can pay good dividends but all too often they are wasted. Many exhibitors will give them to their sales representatives with instructions to distribute them on their calls. This would appear to be a natural way but it makes no real contribution to potential new business. One way used with success by seasoned exhibitors is as follows:

- List all the known users of the product into three categories:

  1. Those who are regular customers already.
  2. Those who are known and have been approached but up to now have not become customers for some reason.
  3. Those who are known but have not been approached.

It will immediately be seen that groups 2 and 3 are clearly the people that could be most profitable and to whom a concentrated approach should be made. An effective way is to send personal letters to named individuals in group 2 suggesting that the recipients may find it useful to see the new range of products being offered for their industry and suggesting a time and date that you have pencilled in your diary for them to visit your stand – and enclosing a personal invitation ticket. This personalised letter should be signed by a director or senior executive. Such invitations do attract a good reply ratio and experience has shown that the replies will fall into the following categories:

- 'Cannot manage the suggested time; can another date be made?'
- 'Not personally visiting the fair this year but could another person visit?'
- 'Not able to leave the office at this time; could you visit me at this office?'

All of these replies can be seen as positive and could lead to an enquiry from a newcomer. All orders from new customers are profitable!

Group 3 prospects should be approached in the same manner if enough executive time is available but group 2 prospects are much better since some background history should be available which can be used by the interviewer.

In practice it is useful to have the background notes about previous meetings. Psychologically, the prospect will be impressed that a director or senior executive has bothered to invite him by name for a special meeting to explain the products and has also demonstrated a good background knowledge of him and the company. It suggests that this is a company that cares about their clients. This does mean that your directors and senior executives will have very busy days at the show with almost continuous half-hour appointments throughout the fair. It also requires competent secretarial research and preparation together with good on-site reception staff to ensure that the expected visitor is correctly received. The day dairy must be maintained at one hundred per cent accuracy.

The mailing lists will also benefit from this sorting process. There is no reason why representatives should not invite their regular customers as well but they should beware of spending too much time chatting about old times. New enquiries and new business are more valuable!

## BROCHURES AND LEAFLETS

There will usually be a requirement for leaflets, brochures and other descriptive or corporate material. Much of this may be drawn from stock but some special exhibition material could well be needed. Previous years' attendance figures should provide an indication of the likely quantities needed. Do ensure that this print material goes to people who really want it, not 'leaflet collectors'. It is advisable to have it under cover within easy reach of staff who can hand them out as required. Photographs of new products that have been used in your press releases could also be available for those customers who are interested in them.

Enquiry pads or cards should be carried by all staff working on the stand, preferably on their person – *never* left loose on a table or worktop. They should be completed conscientiously and always sent to the head office daily so that they can be dealt with quickly, not left for several weeks. If a reply cannot be done by return, one should certainly be sent within 7-10 days maximum. Nothing annoys a potential customer more than to have to wait weeks for a price or proposal after having made an enquiry. Unfortunately this seems to happen all too often with UK manufacturers. Trade fair enquiries from potential new clients should always have top priority.

## OPENING DAYS

The first open day or part of it is often used as a Press day when the general public is excluded. The manager should brief his staff to be aware of the importance of Press enquiries and decide who should handle them. Competent Press officers should always be present on Press day. They could personally know many of the journalists and editors present. Radio and TV journalists may also be present although their producers will usually contact exhibitors in advance if they want to make a recording on any of the stands. Enterprising PR people representing various companies will have contacted producers prior to the opening day to endeavour to obtain a mention or showing.

VIPs and personalities may tour the exhibition, usually accompanied by the organiser. Good preparatory work by your PR manager can help to ensure that your stand is on any such 'walkabout'. You can, of course, engage your own personality to visit your stand, in which case this should be well publicised to all the media and radio and television producers. Tell the exhibition organiser and the press office if you are doing this: they can help with car parking and security. Also, do not forget to brief the official photographer in good time and describe the type of photographs you would like to achieve. Then give them a free hand – they are very experienced and have an eye for the type of picture you want. If you have your own professional press officer, that person should be present also. Everyone should be prepared for the unexpected visitor such as a company VIP appearing without prior warning.

## THE COST

It is in the interest of the organisers of the fair to ensure that the event is well publicised and to that end they will spend part of the exhibition space income that you pay to make sure this happens. For example, a trade fair might allocate 10 per cent of the income while on public events they could very well allocate as much as 50 per cent. This is obviously why the space charges are very much higher at public shows. They need more publicity to attract the public, especially if times are hard. Television advertising (the popular medium for public events) is expensive by comparison with trade journal advertising.

Since exhibitions and trade shows help trade journals sell more advertising space, such journals will normally support exhibitions strongly – indeed, some exhibition organisers have large publishing interests as well. This helps the exhibition to create greater interest in the particular trade or industry to which it is appealing. At the same time, individual exhibitors will want to be associated with the mainstream effort and will also probably advertise in the special exhibition issues.

Exhibitors will typically devote about 10 to 12 per cent of their exhibition budget to stand promotion and publicity for the average trade show. For this amount they should achieve reasonable results. Much can be achieved by thoughtful planning and using methods that are effective without being costly. (For public events these figures can increase greatly.)

## ORGANISERS' PROMOTIONAL AIDS

Most organisers will have various aids available to their standholders in the form of car stickers, posters, exhibition logo stickers, book matches, beermats, etc. Many of these are issued free; some may be at special prices for items being merchandised at public and 'Pop' type shows, and may include T shirts, photographs, pens, pencils, records, video tapes, etc. Study the list of available items and take advantage of those which are free and can benefit your company. All exhibitors should use the 'See our stand at the exhibition' stickers which the organiser will supply. They should be put on all correspondence as a matter of course.

Some exhibitors hold competitions for major prizes at public exhibitions and it may well be worth approaching the organisers to ascertain if they would like to be associated with such an event. In this way, greater prominence can be given to the idea.

## UPDATE BUDGET AND PROGRESS SCHEDULE

The budget and progress schedule must be updated with the complete publicity cost and information. If this work has been done by the publicity department, they must ensure that the EM is kept fully informed of all developments. If the company advertising agency does this work they also should send details of any costs so that the EM may add them to his records.

*Large numbers of potential buyers can see and compare products in one place. The Motor Show at the National Exhibition Centre. (Photograph by Ted Edwards, courtesy of the NEC.)*

# 7

# AT THE EVENT

Exhibitions and trade fairs have varying build-up periods. If they are located in a major venue, the organiser will normally provide adequate time to build the stand. In hotels, where a ballroom or function room may be used, the time may not be so generous because of following functions and 'shell scheme' stand-fitting will generally be used to save time. It is not uncommon for exhibitors to have just the prior evening to prepare. If the event is timed to open at 10 am, total pre-show preparation is absolutely necessary – midnight working is common.

## PRE-EXHIBITION BUILD-UP

Larger events will normally allow between some five and fourteen days to prepare, depending on the complexity of the particular show. If there are large numbers of complicated purpose-built stands then a longer period will be allowed than for an all shell-scheme show. Stand builders usually reckon to complete a typical shell scheme within three to four days and then the exhibitor has to provide the interior dressing exhibits and products.

Most exhibition organisers state in their rules and regulations that the proposed stand design must be submitted for approval and that it must be capable of being built in the limited time available. If an organiser had doubts when the design was submitted he would have discussed these with the exhibitor or his designer and builder. He may reject the design if he is not convinced that it can be built in the given time. For multi-storied constructions written approval will be required from the borough surveyor, building inspector or similar authority for the relevant district and often the fire authority and Health and Safety Inspectorate (as discussed in Chapter 5.) For this reason exhibition organisers ask that such stand designs be submitted early so that they can obtain the necessary approvals. The value of appointing an exhibition designer (as discussed in Chapter 3) can now be clearly seen. The organiser will have greater confidence if he knows your stand is being supervised by a qualified exhibition designer.

The standfitter will normally move onto site on the first building day to unload floor sections, walls and stock materials and commence the building programme. He will bring any finished prefabricated display units and set pieces when the preliminary work has been done so that he can put them into their final position without double handling. While this is going on the electricians will be running mains, plumbers putting down pipework, with the carpet layers following very closely behind. This is a highly planned operation and it is not a good time for the exhibitor or his staff to be on site – better to leave it to the designer and stand contractor to get on with it. Since this book is addressed to all concerned with exhibitions and trade fairs – that is future exhibition organisers, stand builders, venue executives and exhibition managers – a separate chapter will deal with the methods the standfitters employ. After about three days, in a larger show, the stand should be beginning to take shape. It will probably be awaiting its display units, wallpaper and colour and lighting fittings, and the outline will be becoming evident.

Exhibition halls are not unlike warehouses or aircraft

hangars – large empty shell buildings. During the build-up the high entrance doors are nearly always open to allow the contractors to unload their materials. At this time there will be no heating in winter or air-conditioning in summer (it would be totally wasted if there were). The stands and aisles will have no identification, and everything is usually quite untidy. It is easy to become disorientated in a large hall. The cleaners appear not to be able to keep pace with the rubbish that accumulates. Never put a package down next to your stand and leave it unattended – it will almost certainly vanish very quickly! Many pieces of timber with protruding nails will be randomly left on the floor, so always wear tough walking shoes. Women should never wear high-heeled shoes or sandals – tough flat shoes or boots are the only sensible footwear for what is effectively a building site. Increasingly, exhibition sites where heavy exhibits and multi-story construction are being built require that 'hard-hats' are worn, especially early on in the build-up.

Standfitters will endeavour to keep to a realistic schedule. They never have as much time as they would really like so they do not appreciate being held up on site with unnecessary queries. If you have a question, discuss it with your designer or the standfitter's site representative, not the working operatives. They work to their written specification and drawings and will not deviate unless instructed by their chief or their site representative.

If the EM has not carried out an earlier site survey (as recommended in Chapter 5) it is advisable to study the floor plan before going onto site and acquainting yourself with the position of the various services and facilities such as toilets (not all are in use at build-up), first aid, canteen and snack bars, security office, telephone enquiries, hall manager, hall electrician and the various enquiry offices for stand catering, floor covering, furniture hire, signwriting, fireman's and Press office. It is likely that you will need to visit one or more of these at some time during your period at the exhibition. Experienced exhibition managers save a great amount of time and footwork by knowing the location of these essential services.

Aim to complete your stand by lunch-time of the day preceding the opening of the show. Chairmen and chief executives have a habit of requiring difficult last-minute changes. These should be discouraged so far as it is possible – if the particular item was not planned or noticed earlier it probably is not very important or worth the high last-minute cost.

# STATUTORY REQUIREMENTS – FIRE, HEALTH AND SAFETY

Before the exhibition opens, the fire and health and safety inspectors will inspect the complete show. Their duty is to ensure that the event is safe in every respect, and only when they have given their clearance can the event open to the public or trade visitor. The rules and regulations governing all aspects of fire requirements and health and safety needs are always fully stated by the show organiser. Professional exhibition designers and standbuilders follow them as a matter of course to ensure the safety and comfort of everyone involved at the exhibition. Fire inspectors will particularly look for fire traps – the gaps between stands which could become filled with rubbish, boxes, papers, wrappings and similar material that a carelessly discarded match or cigarette end could easily ignite.

Paper and card and unfireproofed materials should never be used. If they are the inspector will require them to be removed before permitting the show to open. The exhibition industry has an extremely good safety record. Although a great amount of timber is used the statutory requirements concerning fireproofing are strictly observed by all established standfitting companies. If a newcomer appears to be in danger of breaking the rules he will soon be told.

Health and safety inspectors have a comprehensive list of requirements which will be stated in the exhibition rules and regulations. They are meticulous where the preparation of food and drink and other catering details are concerned. For example, two washing points will be required in an exhibition stand kitchen – one for washing hands, the other for washing cups, plates, glasses, etc. Hot and cold running water is also required. It is advisable to study and observe the regulations carefully to avoid problems on the stand later.

## DRESSING THE STAND

When the standfitter has finished building most of the stand, the placing of exhibits and general stand dressing can commence. This is usually a most frustrating period. It is always difficult to park your transport near enough to your stand where you would prefer it to be, and if you need cranage or handling equipment to off-load heavy exhibits the lifting services always seem to be late. In fact, lifting contractors do a quite remarkable job. At most exhibitions many of the exhibitors will not have had the foresight to prebook the lifting contractor, but expect to organise it at the drop of a hat on site! This contributes more than any other factor to the delay that the more thoughtful exhibitors suffer. Many lifting contractors are now surcharging late on-site orders in an effort to eliminate such delays.

It is always advisable to return packing cases and similar material to your factory and bring them back on the 'pull-out' day. If you have loose wrappings and paper it helps everyone if this is disposed of into one or two large boxes or bags rather than scattered over the aisle. It also helps to speed the organiser's cleaning-up operation which will be happening at the same time.

## SECURITY

Security is always a problem when stand dressing is taking place. Often the biggest security risk is from other exhibitors – particularly your competitors! Never leave parcels or goods unattended on the stand or in the gangways. Always have at least one person on the stand – particularly at lunch time when many thefts occur. If the exhibits are small enough have them locked in a secure store. Secure should mean solid – not a muslin ceiling – with padlocks or mortise locks, not simple Yale locks, and a reasonably solid door.

Most exhibitions and trade fairs have security guards patrolling on the 'dressing day' and at night. They cannot easily spot a thief if he appears to be working on your stand during daytime but at night they will certainly challenge and usually request identification. Newer exhibition venues also have video cameras that scan the halls by night. These are remotely controlled from the security room and can film a theft taking place. Nightsheets are not considered to be an aid to good security since they provide hiding places for interlopers when the guards are patrolling.

## APPROACHING VISITORS AND BUYERS

The stand or sales manager has briefed the stand staff (he should have done this the evening before), everyone knows their stand 'sales station' – everyone should be in position at least 15 minutes before the opening time – and the first visitors will soon arrive. How should they be approached?

The salesperson should first discreetly note the product that appears to interest visitors and then approach them with an appropriate comment product such as 'This router is new to our range since many companies have requested its new features', or 'We have a whole selection of sizes if this is of interest to you', or 'By the way, my name is Smith, I'd be glad to help you in any way that I can'. This type of approach is positive and helpful, and seen to be so – much more so than the commonly used but ineffective 'Can I help you?', to which there is no positive reply.

It is essential to ascertain the visitor's name, position and company as early as possible. It is not a good idea to provide your competitors with valuable information through idle chatter; they also walk around the show stands and ask questions! If the visitor is a journalist he should be introduced to your press or publicity executive, as discussed Chapter 6.

Many buyers from overseas have a habit of arriving at the show very early in the day; sometimes they will be walking the aisles as the daily opening announcement is being made. They also often stay late and will approach an exhibitor as the closing announcement is being made. Almost every exhibition organiser can tell a story about the 'biggest order taken at the exhibition at one minute past the opening hour or just as the staff were planning to depart for the day'.

This book will not deal at length with exhibition sales techniques, but here we should again emphasise the purpose of an exhibition:

- To show the company's goods, products and services
- To elicit positive enquiries and provide helpful information to potential customers
- To ensure that all enquiries receive prompt 'follow-up' material and courteous attention
- To ensure that any Press enquiry receives reliable non-restricted information which will not embarrass the firm.

If all this is achieved the exercise will have been worthwhile.

## STAFF TIDINESS

At a busy exhibition a stand can very quickly become untidy. Dirty cups, saucers and plates should be cleared when the visitors depart, ashtrays should be emptied frequently, the stand should continue to look inviting at the end of the day, not like a refuse dump. It is all too easy to let this happen, and the EM or stand manager should constantly emphasise the value of good housekeeping.

Staff will get tired: they should be allowed breaks when they can sit and relax away from the 'business end' of the stand, either in a staff room built into the stand or one of the cafes or restaurants within the venue. In no circumstances should they lounge around on the stand, as this does not create a good impression. We have all seen the representative asleep on his stand or a staff group having a private chat – hardly likely to inspire a new customer. Staff should be discouraged from smoking on the stand. Many people find this offensive.

Also, do not forget to replenish supplies. Brochures and leaflets quickly run out. Catering supplies should also be ordered a day in advance.

## THE AFTERMATH

The EM or stand manager should make notes of improvements that could be made for the next show, as he or she notices them. For example, was the stand position ideal, did we really need a larger stand or a greater display area? Were there enough sales stations? Was the supply of literature adequate? Was the lounge area large enough? What were the weaknesses and strengths of the stand?

After the stand has been cleared and while the event is clear in everyone's mind it is useful to have an open discussion at which everyone who participated can contribute their ideas or criticisms. This will form the basis of the requirements for the next show stand. While management will always decide what they want to achieve, the staff who operate the stand can often indicate the best way of achieving those objectives. With this information the EM and/or stand manager can write his final report.

Within two or three months from the end of the exhibition it should also be possible to arrive at a provisional figure showing the number of enquiries received from both old and new clients, the value of those enquiries, and the state of the follow-ups. This information will be helpful when planning future sales strategy and in arriving at a budget and plan for the next exhibition.

It will also be useful to analyse the treatment of the exhibition sales enquiries that were sent through to the sales office back at base. Were these handled quickly? What was the speed of response from the enquirer? Did the base sales office have all the information they needed from the stand representative? Would any other information be helpful to the record keepers? Could the company enquiry form be improved in any way so far as they were concerned? These may seem unimportant at first glance but what better time to examine these questions than when the system has just been tested?

# 8

# EXHIBITING OVERSEAS

No book dealing with exhibitions and trade fairs would be complete without mention of overseas events. We are constantly being reminded we are now part of Europe. The possibility of exhibiting at overseas trade fairs should therefore be included in any overall marketing effort.

Many manufacturers interested in exporting their products already recognise the value of overseas trade fairs. Continental European countries have many established shows that are highly rated by the trade buyers who attend. The waiting list of intending exhibitors in the top fairs is proof of this. Reviews and reports of these events can be seen in the industry journals and often in the quality dailies and weekly press. Information can also be obtained from trade associations and Chambers of Commerce. The largest of these maintain lists of trade events world-wide.

The international exhibition association *Union des Foires Internationales* (UFI) accepts to its affiliation only those trade fairs which have been thoroughly vetted by experienced and impartial assessors and which have proved over a period of time – usually at least three events – that they do attract the quality of both exhibitor and trade visitor that is stated in the promotional material of the event. This will include a minimum proportion of overseas exhibitors or visitors. The UFI is recognised by governments, the EU and many trade associations as being a quality organisation which recognises only those events that are worthwhile. They have members in virtually every country.

In Britain, the DTI Overseas Promotion Support Scheme will sometimes provide joint venture assistance to a trade association whose members are proposing to exhibit at a recognised trade fair. This assistance can amount to a contribution towards space rents, shipping and transport charges, simple shell scheme standfitting and the services of an interpreter on site. Interested trade associations should always make early enquiries to the exhibition organiser or his agent to ascertain if such assistance might be available. Similar assistance is also available for some inward and outward trade missions.

Appendix 3 describes some of the services available to UK exporters. The EU at Brussels also have assistance 'Packages' for their members. The British Commercial Consulate in the country concerned can provide information. The DTI overseas promotions support branch in the UK will also provide much helpful advice and literature.

In some cities and towns where major trade fairs are held (particularly in continental Europe) the British consulate will have staff who specialise in some of the subjects of the fairs. It is always wise to make early contact with the consulate in the town or city that is hosting the event. They usually have a fund of valuable knowledge.

Companies intending to exhibit overseas for the first time would be wise to send their export or marketing manager to reconnoitre the territory they are considering the year prior to the event, if they can. As well as enabling them to obtain on-the-spot information about the fair and its visitors, they can also meet overseas agents, as well as commercial staff at the local consulate. Hotels can be vetted, restaurants inspected and a general survey of the area undertaken.

Many of the continental European trade fairs are very heavily booked from year to year, and it may be necessary to join a waiting list. Some have a ballot system and it may not be possible to achieve the desired stand position in the first year. Some allocate certain halls or pavilions or groups of stand spaces by nationality to the various participating countries, so they will be together. This can be helpful to the buyer.

First-time visitors are often surprised at the size of some of the events, and continental Europe has some very large exhibition venues. Trade fairs have always been popular for the European buyer and visitor; more so than British trade fairs are to British visitors.

Most towns and cities in Europe fund their own exhibition complexes from the municipal treasury and the revenue they generate benefits the whole city. In some towns, hotels and restaurants are required to levy a small tax on their charges at the time of trade fairs for the benefit of the town and exhibition hall upkeep expenses. In this respect they have a great advantage over the UK where venues cannot compete with halls and facilities of such size since they need to be funded by the private sector. (One exception is the City of Birmingham, which has the National Exhibition Centre as well as the International Conference Centre. )

## PROCEDURES

Assuming the decision has been taken to exhibit at a foreign event, the question arises: what has to be done that is different from UK fairs?

In fact there is very little difference. All exhibitions and trade fairs follow much the same format wherever they are held, but in the case of overseas events it is essential that all arrangements are made in adequate time and nothing be forgotten. It is not so convenient to rush back to the office or factory!

Space should be booked as early as possible, which in practice may mean booking for the subsequent, not the next, show which could be three years distant. This has some advantages. It would be possible to visit the fair a year before and note what the competition is doing and in particular observe the nationality of the predominant visitors attending, what language is most popular (at all mainland European shows a number of languages are spoken but French, German, Spanish or Italian, and English are used widely). Notice also which appears to be the busiest hall and the busiest show area. If the plan is to exhibit within a country group take note of how other national groups are working out – what mistakes are being made, what languages are being used for the captioning. These impressions are going to be very useful when planning your own stand.

On your travels around the show you may even notice work carried out by a local standfitter who you consider to be good. Take a note of his name and address, it may be useful. You may come across a really good interpreter (they are like gold dust). If you have already appointed your agent he should be able to introduce you to potential clients who are at the fair. Spend several days and evenings socialising because a lot of your future potential customers are going to be there and quite possibly some of your existing clients.

Visit the organising and Press office. Find out the daily attendance figures and the breakdown by country. Later the organiser should provide you with a breakdown showing the trades or professions of the visitors together with other relevant factors about the attendance. Is one day more important than another? If you have company experts who have limited time to visit, they would wish to attend on the most important days.

If you can gain access into the Press Office find out which journalists – from trade journals as well as international media – are attending. Everyone is expected to sign the visitors' book, so this is easy to find out. Look at the Press cuttings, which will indicate what stories have attracted editors. Your own PRO could well attend for this purpose if you are planning a future major presence. The information you glean from this visit is going to be invaluable to you and the company and you will not feel lost when you arrive at the venue later.

# APPOINTING THE CONTRACTORS

After the space is booked the organiser or UK agent will provide information concerning details such as hotels, special airline fares and arrangements, recommended shippers and forwarding agents, approved standfitters, electricians, plumbers, furniture hirers, interpreters and temporary exhibition staff together with much other information. He will also send you the exhibition rules and regulations, forms to be completed for your electricity supply, water, telephones, car parking, staff entry passes and visitor passes together with a mass of other information. The same procedures that were followed for a UK exhibition will apply. Once again it becomes the duty of your exhibition manager to put together a coherent budget, have it approved and prepare a progress schedule and work through it as the work and timing dictates.

Most of the budget items will be as the UK version set out in Chapter 4 (see pages 31-32). The big difference will be in sections 3 and 4 relating to stand building and associated services. If it is a very large trade fair it is likely that one or more British standfitters are proposing to work there. In this event, it could be easier for you to employ their services. Cost-wise there is little difference if they have several stands or pavilions to build. Whether you employ British or foreign standfitters, it is easier to order all requirements through one standfitter. He is on site and can do his own chasing as necessary. He will also know the best and most reliable fitters to employ. It may cost a little more, but it removes the worry factor.

# SHIPPING AND DOCUMENTATION

Shipping dates should be noted very carefully. They may be some time away, but if a shipping date is missed it will almost certainly involve extra expense, possibly requiring air transport where sea or land transport could have been used. Make sure that all documentation is complete and correct in all details. If the customs officials require a bond, make sure this has been arranged. Customs officers can be difficult if the paperwork is not in order and exhibitions and trade fairs will not wait! Specialist firms experienced in arranging exhibition and trade fair shipments are available in the UK. They will look after all exhibition documentation – which is different in many instances from general shipping procedures. Use these specialists in preference to general shippers and forwarding agents – they cost no more.

# INSURANCE

Ensure that everything and everybody going to the exhibition is insured, including the stand and all its contents. The goods should be insured from the day they leave the factory continuing through the time they are in transit, through the show period and dismantling up to the time they arrive back at the factory. The stand itself should be insured from the time building commences until it is dismantled.

The staff involved should have travel and medical insurance appropriate for the country in question. For example, Africa and Asia will need a more comprehensive medical insurance than most European countries. Certain destinations – some Middle Eastern areas, for example – may require additional travel insurance against other risks.

# PASSPORTS AND VISAS

Check at an early date if visas are required and make early application if needed. Are staff passports valid? If vaccinations and inoculations are necessary arrange these well ahead of time. Some people suffer bad after-effects lasting up to a couple of weeks. A staff member suffering with fever is not much use on the stand. Once again, check that a key member of staff is not getting married or having a baby at the critical time.

# INTERPRETERS

Particular attention should be paid to the appointment of an interpreter. This person will be very important to you during the show. The impression that he or she gives to those visiting your stand will be the one they will remember. Ask your agent to ensure that the person has a working understanding of your company and knowledge of its products and philosophy. If possible, let the interpreter spend a few days at your works or office, meeting people and understanding your products. The ideal situation is for all staff to be able to speak the main languages fluently – but this is rarely possible.

# PUBLICITY PR AND PROMOTION

All promotional material, leaflets and brochures should be written in the language of the host country and extracts in the four major languages, English, French, German, and Spanish or Italian. With Spanish or Italian, choose the language of the majority at that exhibition. (In practice, nationals of Italy or Spain tend to understand the other language or will speak French or English.) Press notices should always be succinct and preferably in the four chosen languages, at least in extract form. If this is not possible, then they should be in the host language.

If the exhibition press staff need to, they will translate any material they wish to use.

Local knowledge of favoured trade journals is helpful and for this reason your local agent should be involved. If you do not have such a person, the facilities offered by the commercial consul at the British embassy or consulate should be sought.

Direct mail and exhibition invitations should be sent to potential customers with the cooperation of your overseas sales agent. They should always be written in the language of the recipient.

It may be beneficial to arrange to arrange a press reception to launch your company or its products. This can be in a private room or suite at a hotel or maybe on the stand itself.

Many British buyers visit overseas fairs so why not invite them as well? It can do no harm for them to realise that yours is an expansive company.

## EXHIBITION STAFF

All sales staff should have a good knowledge of the forward prices of the products that are displayed – in the currency of the person to whom they are speaking. Staff should also ensure that promised quotations are sent promptly; in practice this should mean within about 7-10 days. Using a fax can speed communications.

## HOTEL AND SUITCASE SHOWS – OVERSEAS AND UK

An economical method of exhibiting smaller products is by hotel room displays. These are becoming increasingly popular for products such as consumer electronic goods, for example. A group of manufacturers will agree to get together in a hotel at a certain day or days and each take a room to lay out their products and samples using collapsible display units and caption boards. The event will be publicised jointly to the industry through their trade publications and direct mail invitations. Sometimes they can virtually take over the whole hotel. Hotels are very happy to accommodate these manufacturers since as well as taking bedrooms for exhibition use, they also take other bedrooms for accommodation. The restaurants and bars also benefit from this business. They are not very sophisticated events but they are not expensive either. Some of these trade groups may amount to one or two hundred exhibiting manufacturers and can attract large trade audiences over a period of several days. They are particularly popular in the USA and becoming increasingly so elsewhere, including the UK.

## USEFUL HINTS

Electrical supplies vary throughout the world and if working exhibits are envisaged it is vital that the right information is known in advance. The British Standards Institute provides details in a booklet entitled 'Survey of Supply Voltage Throughout the World' (reference number TH20338 and obtainable from the BSI). The BSI has been investigating the various foreign markets and gathering information on technical legislation and the practices and procedures adopted. This information can be obtained from the BSI in publications under their general heading of 'Technical help to exporters'.

It is generally accepted that the structural and fire and safety standards enforced at the London exhibition venues are the most stringent in the world and if these standards are adopted for work carried out in all other exhibitions problems should be negligible.

All countries have their own different approach toward exhibitions. Whilst it is not possible to be absolutely specific, the following general observations have been noted by the author over a number of years.

The UK, continental Europe and Scandinavia pay great

attention to safety and correct fireproofing of all materials used in stand building. These electrical and structural regulations and requirements should always be respected. The labour force is experienced and mostly trade union, but not restrictively so. Shipping and forwarding is reliable and efficient providing the documentation is correct.

The USA follows similar safety rulings and interpretations to those used in Europe, but their labour force is totally unionised and tends to be restrictive. Without the right 'ticket' progress is virtually impossible. Many US exhibitions still use the 'pipe and drape' booth system (rather like hemmed curtain fabrics threaded or draped on metal tubes). It is a quick and simple system allowing fast preparation without ambitious display ideas, but the European style of more elaborate stand fitting is being adopted with various modular systems now available. It should be noted that US shipping and customs procedures at trade fairs and exhibitions can be very slow.

In most of the Third-World countries standards are improving all the time. As a general rule, they follow the European pattern but not always to the same standards. Shipping and transportation can be difficult, so always allow extra time in hand. Product clearance in particular can be very difficult. It is never entirely clear whether the delay is caused by shippers, packers, forwarding agents or customs, but tipping never fails to ease the process: in some countries it is a recognised procedure and no matter what you may think, do ensure that gratuities are included in your budget.

The developed countries in Africa and Asia follow virtually the same pattern as Europe. Customs and shipping are well organised and it is only in the less-developed countries that problems will be encountered.

## OVERSEAS CONTINGENCY

When budgeting for overseas exhibitions always include a larger contingency allowance than for UK exhibitions and if the event is in a Third World country allow a particularly large contingency on the transportation, shipping and clearance budget, including the return load out of the country. It is advisable to consult your local agent for advice.

# 9

# THE CONTRACTORS

The role of the standfitters is crucial. Without them the exhibition will not be built. The setting they provide will be the base for you and your products. Like general builders, they come in all shapes and sizes, some large some small, some good some bad, but predominantly they are specialist joinery houses that can carry out all types of joinery work from erecting stud partitioning for temporary buildings to the highest standards of display and cabinet-making. They can build, decorate and completely furnish an exhibition house in about fourteen days – as those who have exhibited at a 'Homes' type exhibition will know.

## METHODS AND LABOUR EMPLOYED

Most workshops have different groups of tradespeople for different types of work. Some operatives prefer to build shell-scheme stands on site, others prefer the delicate benchwork required for elegant display and high-class cabinet-making. Many standfitters are also concerned with general display work and often with shopfitting. These aspects all complement each other and help the contractor to achieve a balanced flow of work.

The tradespeople who work in the industry are highly skilled and, consequently, highly paid. Employers cannot afford to have this valuable labour standing around doing nothing, nor can they 'hire and fire' since it could be difficult to replace key craftsmen. Hence they endeavour to maintain a full programme of work by spreading their net over kindred interests.

Other trades apart from joiners are also involved in the final exhibition stand and will be found in the workshops from time to time. Most standfitting companies also employ machinists, labourers, progress chasers, storekeepers and drivers. Some may have a spray-shop and operator, particularly if they handle a lot of display work. They may also have an art studio where photo mounting, tinting and general artwork can be carried out. Silk-screen printing is normally bought in but sometimes a production artist may find it better to use this technique for a one-off exhibition operation to achieve a certain effect. Trades such as painters, signwriters, electricians, metal-workers, carpet-layers, floral decorators and animators are often subcontracted out and brought in as required, thus enabling the stand builder to call on the best resources available. It would be uneconomic to employ all of these trades on a full-time basis without an enormously large and varied turnover. The stand-building fraternity is comparatively small compared with other industries so everyone in the business knows their competitors' capabilities and where to find any required specialists.

Most of the display work, set pieces, cut-out letters, plinths, counters and other self-standing items are prefinished in the works to ensure a perfect finish and then wrapped and stored until they are needed on site. It is more economical to work this way: quite often a complex exhibition stand or overseas pavilion can be several weeks or even months in preparation at the works.

Electrical pre-fabrication is often be carried out in the stand-fitter's works to ease the electricians' on-site workload. Display pieces will be pre-wired and tested, with a tail left for site connection. Standfitters will always ensure the maximum work is carried out in the workshop. If the stand is particularly complicated, a 'dry' assembly may be carried out to ensure a trouble-free build-up on site. As much painting and decorating work as possible will also be done in the workshop so that the site painter has only to finish off. If timber polishing is required this will be done off-site, protectively wrapped and carefully stored. The only trades not generally involved in the workshop are the carpet and tile layers, furniture hirers, plumbers, telephone engineers and suchlike, whose work is always on site. Time spent on site is always more expensive and never as productive.

During the works preparation many other related functions are being performed. The job specification may have called for special fabrics for curtains, drapes or upholstery, in which case samples have to be obtained and approved. The designer or client may have decided they need special ironmongery or finishes. Purpose-mixed colours or processes take more time to obtain and clients often change their mind when they see them. Specialised electrical fittings or animated effects may be envisaged, and often complicated metal work has to be manufactured. Special effects are being increasingly used and much work can go into them. Quite often the client or designer has visualised a good idea or effect but does not know how to achieve it. This is where the experienced standfitter comes into his own: he will usually know the 'specialist' in a particular area. Much that is seen at today's exhibitions will have been purpose-made for a one-off use.

Most standfitters employ a 'trouble-shooter' who doubles as a progress chaser. Frequently they are also responsible for buying special items. This person must ensure that everything needed on a particular project – whether it is specialist labour or material – is available at the moment that it is needed and that the expense involved is costed into the project.

As the project proceeds through the workshop the various prefabricated sections are passed through to the paintshop and, when complete, wrapped and passed to stores to await despatch on the appropriate day. Once again the progress executive has to note the state of these pieces on the schedule and inform the storeman when the items have to go onto site.

# SHELL SCHEMES

Throughout this book reference is made to 'shell schemes', which are becoming increasingly popular. Shell schemes are like ready-to-wear outfits and are economically priced whereas bespoke outfits, made to measure, obviously cost more. The approach to shell scheme work is different from that of bespoke. Joiners engaged on shell schemes have an entirely different outlook on life: they enjoy being on site and working against the clock. Exhibitions using shell schemes require the stands to be completed quickly, sometimes in just a few hours. Even the larger shows will rarely allow builders more than four days to build the layout.

There are two basic styles of shell schemes: traditional and modular. The traditional schemes are being steadily replaced by modular schemes which can be erected much faster, thus saving costs. Modular components are also very much lighter in weight.

## *TRADITIONAL SHELL SCHEMES*

Traditional schemes comprise the following elements:

*Stock panels*, 8 or 9 ft high (2.74 or 2.5 m), usually 4 ft wide (2.20 m) with smaller 'make-up' panels. They are constructed from a framework of '2 × 1' softwood timber batons faced with either one ¼ in. thick plywood or hardboard sheet. They can be provided with one side faced (single-sided stock panels) or both sides faced (double-sided stock panels).

*Floor flats.* Older stock consists of 6 × 2 ft units constructed from 1 in timber boarding laid on 3 × 2 timber joists, which provide a raised platform 4 in. high. Newer floor stock comprises sheets of chipboard blockboard, masterboard or any other approved timber composite board laid on joists or more commonly cruciforms (small timber crosses 2 or 3 in. thick and about 12 in. long), which can be put into place quickly. Platforms are used mostly for traditional shell schemes; they are rarely used in modular schemes. The platforms are trimmed with 3 or 4 in. high 1 in. thick timber kickboards nailed to the joist ends and painted.

*Fascias* are usually 2 ft or 1.6 ft deep constructed in a similar manner to stock panels. They are often recessed on the inside face to allow a fixing for a muslin ceiling, common in most traditional shell schemes. Fascia supports are 2 in. or 1 in. metal tubes, either square or round, fitted with baseplates and fascia holding brackets.

## MODULAR SHELL SCHEMES

Modular schemes, which have many variations, are popular because of the speed of erection and the consequent saving of

*An Octanorm shell scheme stand showing some interesting variations to the usual fascia treatment and tower supports at the 1988 Hanover Trade Fair. (Designed by the Fairs and Promotions branch of the DTI and built by Beck Exhibitions.)*

expensive build-up days for the exhibition organisers and the exhibitors. They came into general use in the UK in 1975 when the author, as the technical director for the Montgomery group, was asked to find a new, quickly erected but flexible shell scheme for their larger exhibitions. After several months investigating schemes and systems, the 'Octanorm' modular shell scheme was selected. Within a short time it was adopted by many of the major exhibition organisers in the UK. It is widely used in Europe (where it made its original debut) and increasingly so in many other parts of the world. It is a popular choice for firms who want their own permanent stand for use at exhibitions and other presentations. In many ways it resembles a giant Meccano set of parts which, as well as being flexible, are very light. The material used is aluminium plus specially prepared dense, but very strong, composite insert panels which are provided already finished in colour. Nowadays, many copies and variations of lightweight modular schemes are available.

A large variety of optional extra display items can be provided to the exhibitor who wishes to embellish the stand; these are usually provided on hire for the period of the exhibition. Most exhibition stands, shell or bespoke, are provided on hire for the period of the exhibition. The standfitter uses the stock elements – i.e. floors, walls, doors, panels, fascias, supports and the lighting fittings – continuously for successive exhibitions and charges exhibitors a hire rate. This is a more economical proposition for the exhibitor than being charged for new items. The hire items are inspected, renovated and, when necessary, replaced in the periods between shows.

The purpose-made fitments the standfitter prepares for a particular stand can usually be retained by the exhibitor if required, since special items do not always have a reuse value, but units such as counters and shelves, plinths and similar items can be renovated and re-hired. Often much of a stand may have to be destroyed since the standfitters may not have the necessary site time to reclaim materials from used exhibition stands. Labour is expensive and the renovation of materials and subsequent storage for a possible but unknown use is not a viable proposition. Local salvage contractors fare very well from this source.

## OUTSIDE EVENTS

Agricultural shows, garden festivals, fetes, carnivals and many similar events also call for the skills of the standfitter but involve different techniques. Canvas tents and big tops are often used for the structural part of the presentation – for example, at agricultural or air shows such as the Farnborough or Paris Air shows. The canvas is hired in from specialist contractors, but the internal work follows the same principles as used at an indoor event.

Stands that will be in the open often use metal display units to withstand inclement weather. The interiors of some tented structures can be very lavish, as anyone who has attended an up-market garden party will know. Service trunking for electrical energy, water, communication equipment and the like on these sites have to be run quite separately, often large distances, and are not so readily available as in an exhibition hall. Sometimes it is necessary to provide pathways or even tarmac roads.

Stand builders are very flexible and may be called upon to work in many unusual areas. At an agricultural show, for example, it is advisable to provide either platforms or some form of floor protection such as sisal carpeting or coconut matting on individual outdoor event stands. At long-running events consideration should be given to preparing solid bases with drainage for the stands and exhibits. Furniture hirers provide a range of furniture suitable for outside use.

Garden festivals provide the opportunity of using greenhouses and other similar structures. Landscape nurserymen and floral contractors demonstrate their skills in such environments. Carnivals and fetes provide all manner of opportunities for designers and display artists. The design, embellishment and building of carnival floats can give as much enjoyment to the public as to the professionals who build them. A wide range of effects is possible and everyone's ideas are useful; in fact people themselves can become part of the float decoration and contribute to the interest.

## DISPLAY WORK

All exhibition stands will have some display work. It is not possible to describe every type of display technique that is available since there are so many and the list grows as new creative ideas enter the market-place. It should be kept in mind that the whole reason for being at the exhibition is to show goods, products or services and to attract the attention of potential buyers or specifiers.

Smaller products can be shown on shelves, plinths, in show-cases, mounted on panels or suspended. They might even be hidden in the sales office if a degree of commercial secrecy is desired. Larger pieces of machinery may stand in a prepared decorative bed on the floor of the stand. If it has moving parts and is to be demonstrated in a working state it will need protective railing or fencing to prevent accidents. It may need toughened glass screens if grinding or similar operations are involved. Amplification of the demonstrator's voice may be necessary if the machine is noisy.

Photographs of alternative models may be displayed adjacent to a demonstration. They should be wet-mounted onto separate panels which can then be pinned to a wall in the appropriate position. This is useful if the photo panel is to be retained after the exhibition. By wet-mounting (a common process used by most studios) a photoprint can be stretched tight onto a board without bubbles or creases. It is helpful to the viewer to provide a brief caption drawing attention to the finer points in order to stimulate interest and elicit questions. Photographs of the founder or the original factory rarely excite interest unless they are the work of a famous painter or photographer. If the product is uninteresting in appearance it will be the task of the designer or display artist to find a means of enhancing the product interest. For example, a lump of coal or a block of concrete are not greatly eye-catching but if placed onto a vivid red velvet cushion inside a glass showcase edged with a brass frame and illuminated with a low-level spotlight, then they will look more attractive (or at least the trimmings would). An obvious lead-in caption would be 'A jewel of a piece'.

Lighting is all important. Displays or interest features should be well illuminated. Low-voltage spotlights are a most effective light source. They can be adjusted to throw a circle of light the size of the actual item being displayed or to give a general spread of light.

It should be remembered that the ambience of fluorescent light is cold. It can be provided in various tints of white but it does not emit any heat at all whereas tungsten spotlights are warm in every sense. They can transform a product display if well used, but if they are used as a roof lights shining down on people's heads they will cause glare and headaches, and will become a nuisance to visitors and staff alike.

Lighting is a specialised art and proper advice should be sought. Electrical energy can be very expensive at exhibitions and the inexperienced exhibitor can waste a great deal of money.

## ANIMATION AND COLOUR

Movement and colour attract attention. How can the two be put together? Why not start with the staff who are working on the stand? They will be moving all the time. In an earlier chapter we discussed dressing the stand staff in red blazers and grey trousers or skirts. A distinctive costume is a useful start, but all staff should be dressed in the same colours so that the visitor cannot mistake or miss them.

Colour can also be used through floral displays or with coloured lights, perhaps changing colours on different displays or products. Animation specialists have devised many different forms of movement over the years which can be used both for theatrical or trade fair and exhibition use. With the development of improved software, many programs can be devised to run on computers which are increasingly becoming a useful component to use at exhibitions and trade fairs as well as in lavish theatrical productions. Theatre special effects and lighting designers are working more and more in exhibitions and trade fairs, particularly the major events such as Expos and the large public spectaculars that attract large audiences and the revenue to finance the expenditure needed to provide such effects.

Most animation is based on switches and relays, combined with varieties of turntables driven by electric motors, often with variable speed capability. Lights and mirrors can also be used to good effect. Video projection and multi-screens, laser theatres, holograms and talking heads are some of the animation effects commonly being used. In the past spinning rings, 'pepper's ghost', changing captions, various sound effects and water cascades were popular.

Using all these basic techniques animators can create almost any effect. As well as animated and electrical effects exhibition model agencies can now supply specialist staff like walking clowns and robots – indeed, mechanical figures of any desired character – which are especially effective for children's events and promotions.

## PRODUCT LAUNCHES IN-HOUSE AND OTHER PLACES

Standfitters are also required for fitments and displays at company 'in-house' events, either in their own factory or showroom or in a local hotel. The advantages of these venues are apparent if the audience is small. They may be desirable places to which customers will be attracted. The cost of this can be high and the exhibiting company must therefore consider if the expense is justified. At least, they must achieve buyer interest; consumer-orientated companies wishing to attract large store group buyers and similar VIPs may decide to offer the lavish and unusual hospitality that can be provided at such events.

## STUDIO SETTINGS

Most skilled standfitters will periodically receive requests to provide a set. This may be needed for an in-house video or television advertisement or promotional film or maybe a product photo session. The standfitter will normally use his traditional stock panels to create the background and room walls as required and he can do this very quickly. Many standfitters have TV divisions that carry out this type of work for film and television contractors.

## SIGNAGE – POSTERS – TYPOGRAPHY

All signage and typography used in the exhibition must have regard to the distance from which it is to be read. The fascia and top-of-stand signs have to be read from a long distance, so these will need lettering of 300 to 450 mm (1.0 to 1.6 ft) with an open rather than condensed typeface. Mid-distance signage, as seen from one or two aisles away, should be at eye-level

*A busy stand at 'Communication 90' at the World Trade Centre, Singapore. (Photograph provided by Singapore Exhibition Services.)*

with a lettering size of 100 to 150mm (4 to 6 in.).

The product or display caption panels – read from immediately in front of the stand – should preferably be laid out by a typographer. They may have to carry text in two or three languages, each of which could take a varying amount of space. It could be that various parts of the text need to be emphasised.

The typeface to be used should be well considered. Serif letters read more easily if the text is long (Times is a good example), while Univers or similar reads well for headings. It is often useful to have backlit captions. Caption panels can also effectively be 'reversed out'- white on black rather than black on white.

Three-dimensional or animated poster sites are sometimes available within an exhibition complex. These can create great interest amongst the attending audience and, since it is known in advance that viewers have an interest in the products of that particular exhibition, there is no wastage. These sites again illustrate the skills of the display artists within the exhibition industry.

## OFFICES AND REST AREAS

Most stands will need an office, storeroom or lounge/rest area for functional working. The office should be in a discreet part of the stand, totally hidden from the gaze of passers-by and incorporating working areas and power points for computers and other office equipment, telephone and fax. Lighting should be fluorescent and well placed. Furniture should equate to normal office requirements with the addition of sufficient lockable cupboards and other safe storage areas for confidential documents.

If refreshments are to be served, a kitchen must be provided with two sinks and hot and cold running water to conform to the requirements of the Health and Safety Inspectorate (as discussed in an earlier chapter). The visitors' lounge or rest area should preferably not be easily visible since this will encourage 'hangers-on'. Seating should be comfortable but not too much so! Chairs with narrower seats become uncomfortable after about 20 to 30 minutes, a device used to persuade visitors not to stay too long. Furniture hire contractors carry many such types of chairs. Coffee tables, chairs, settees, etc., can be hired in a wide range of colours styles and sizes.

# FIREPROOFING AND SAFETY REGULATIONS

It has already been mentioned that standfitters are required to build to standards dictated by the various authorities. These regulations and requirements vary from area to area, county to county and country to country so every exhibition venue will have its own peculiarities. It is generally accepted that the requirements for London halls are the most exacting in the UK, and possibly in the world, so standfitters normally work to London standards as a matter of course. All materials used must conform to the standards laid down by the fire authority. The fire officer has the authority to submit any material used in building the stand to a flame test. Construction is subject to inspection by the building inspector and the borough surveyor.

It is the exhibition organiser's responsibility to publish all appropriate regulations and provide them to the exhibitors. It is the responsibility of the standfitter to ensure that these regulations and standards are met in the building of the stand. Over the course of many years, the UK exhibition industry has gained an excellent and enviable reputation for safety. These requirements have already been stated, but in view of their importance no excuse is made for emphasising them again. They also apply to any event held in a private hall or venue.

# 10

# EXHIBITION AND TRADE FAIR
# VENUES

## HALLS

Almost every city or town has a hall or building where exhibitions can be held. It may be the town or village hall, the local church hall or another similar building. Any of these could be of sufficient size to house a small craft show or local home type exhibition directed at the local population.

Only the larger exhibition halls and complexes can host the major trade exhibitions – such as London, Birmingham, Manchester, Glasgow and Harrogate. All of these have major exhibition halls with the facilities to handle the weight of vehicle and visitor traffic that such events generate.

Smaller venues are available in Aberdeen, Bristol, Brighton, Bournemouth, and Stoneleigh for agricultural shows. An increasing number of other smaller venues are becoming available for use. These include the many leisure centres at major racecourses, golf clubs, etc., where the indoor space and catering facilities are under-used for much of the time. They can be particularly suitable for private product launches and similar events.

The choice of the exhibition venue will determine the success or failure of the event. The factors the professional organiser evaluates will include:

• The geographical position of the exhibition city or town relative to motorways, major roads and railway stations.
• Is the hall well served by public transport?
• Can overseas visitors and buyers travel easily to the venue from their country?
• Are there adequate hotel rooms and facilities nearby?
• Is adequate parking space for contractors' and exhibitors' commercial vehicles available (and near) to the hall?
• Are there enough private car parking spaces for both exhibition staff and visitors?

These are some of the questions the organiser will consider even before he examines the actual hall and its facilities.

## TRADE SHOWS

Trade shows are usually held at the major exhibition complexes. If they have a space requirement of over 50,000 square metres this effectively means Birmingham, London or Glasgow. These cities have the total facilities that an exhibition or trade show of this size needs.

## VEHICLE FACILITIES

The larger international events attract a lot of road transport from near and far. Most exhibitors and their contractors use this means of transportation to move their exhibits and standfitting materials. Recent calculations have shown that for an exhibition of 50-70,000 square metres – which in the UK would be accommodated at the National Exhibition Centre, Olympia, Earls Court, or the Scottish Exhibition Centre, around 300 vehicles could descend on the exhibition hall on the first day of building. All these are intent on unloading their vehicles – lorries, container trucks, low loaders and vans – and then returning to their base with the minimum of delay. In the case of very heavy exhibits and machinery, cranage and forklift facilities will have to be ready and available to move exhibits into the required position in the exhibition.

The timing of all these movements is unpredictable. Some may arrive the night before the first permitted build-up day, in which case they will require on-site parking and nearby accommodation, canteen and toilet facilities for the crew. Others will arrive at the crack of dawn on the first building day. These will need marshalling by stewards to avoid traffic congestion.

The site 'movement' manager works in close cooperation with the exhibition hall manager, aided by personal radio telephones which are also held by the individual hall managers listening out so that all concerned can contribute at the appropriate time, should the need arise. The aim of every exhibition manager is to clear the traffic to its correct position on site as quickly and safely as possible.

The traffic flow inside the exhibition building also has to be carefully controlled. Vehicles are often allowed inside the venue on the first building day to unload heavy exhibits onto the stand but on subsequent building days only small forklift trucks and essential cranage may be allowed access to the hall. Hand trollies are often used to transport stand sections and miscellaneous display material and exhibits into the building. Main gangways are rarely wider than 3 metres and subsidiary and cross-aisles can be as narrow as 2 metres – not wide enough for normal road transport to negotiate turns. Exhibition forklift trucks and small cranes can turn within their own width.

Most exhibitions employ a one-way system both outside and inside the building. Quite often the perimeter roads are so arranged that they encircle the exhibition halls, with parking areas or lay-bys at various intervals, usually adjoining an entrance/exit door. This enables late arrivals access at a point reasonably near to their stand.

Aisles can become congested very quickly with all stand-holders intent on unwrapping and building their material as quickly as possible. Firm control is necessary to ensure the aisles remain passable. Cleaners remove rubbish at a fast rate, and many exhibitors who have carelessly placed a package in a gangway have found it missing when they returned.

Vehicle congestion and illegal parking are among the biggest problems an exhibition manager has to face. In modern exhibition buildings (those built from 1970 onwards), the goods and vehicle entrance doors are generally around 5.5 metres high and 6.0 metres wide, arranged so that they face each other, allowing vehicles to drive in on one side of the building and out of the other. A wide gangway – usually not less than 3.0 metres – is left through the exhibition floor joining these doors so that in the event of a fire or other emergency, a fire appliance can enter the building unimpeded. Exhibition and event buildings will usually have several sets of these facing doors. The modern exhibition hall has doors with enough tolerance or clearance to accommodate any vehicle that travels on a motorway.

Roadways within an exhibition complex should always be clearly sign-posted so that drivers have no difficulty in finding the required building or hall. Signage in the larger centres should be in appropriate European languages – usually English and French. Exhibition complexes control and police their own roadways and parking areas, but those that are located on major highways or in a city centre do have a difficult parking problem. The larger venues, like the NEC, also have their own private police or security force, usually controlled by an ex-senior police officer.

## GENERAL HALL SERVICES

Landlords and owners normally provide all services that exhibition organisers and their shows require – indeed, if a new service is required they will usually be very happy to provide it since renting out facilities is part of their business and produces revenue. They will also provide the hall staff the exhibition or trade fair organiser needs like gatemen and security guards, cleaners, labourers, car-parking attendants, firemen, electricians, plumbers and any other staff needed for the exhibition and the complex.

Catering services and associated facilities and hire services are also available from the venue owners. Wines, spirits, beers, coffee, tea, cigarettes, etc., as well as glasses and cups and saucers can all be supplied; indeed, the venue rental agreement usually states that only the venue owner may provide these. Some exhibitions will require clubrooms for groups of visitors and others may have a series of conferences in conjunction with their exhibition. These are facilities which most venues can provide and are accustomed to handling.

Sometimes a proportion of the rateable value of the building may also be payable by the tenant (the exhibition organiser) so he is obliged to add this cost to the show overheads and charge proportionately to the exhibitor on a square metre basis.

## FLOOR LOADING AND TECHNICAL SERVICES

The floor loading at modern UK venues is usually rated at 20 tonnes per square metre. This meets the requirements of most indoor exhibitions.

Electricity, gas, water and waste, compressed air, telephone and CCTV services are usually provided via walkway tunnels and cross-over ducting systems which are located on all stands. Air-conditioning and heating is operated by the venue at the level required by the exhibition or event that is in tenancy.

Electricity in the UK is normally either 220-240 volt single phase or 415 volt three-phase. Connection to the venue mains is carried out by the venue electrician at a stated published charge. Similarly, gas, water waste and compressed air services are connected to the main supply by the venue engineer or plumber at published rates. Telephones are connected to supply lines permanently located and maintained by the telephone authorities. These are either BT or Mercury, whichever is authorised by the venue owners. CCTV distribution is provided either by the venue authority or their nominated contractor. In all cases, use of these services and connection thereto can only be at the discretion of the venue managers.

Hall lighting varies from venue to venue. The National Exhibition Centre in Birmingham, for example, has a natural light source and artificial background lighting level up to 400 lux. Most venues will not permit any tenant to tamper with the roof and ceiling fixtures, or indeed any other fittings. Some will permit hanging signs but such work must always be carried out by their own riggers.

# RECEPTION AND REGISTRATION

The reception and registration areas are normally situated at the entrance to the individual halls, and at multi-hall complexes they are at the main entrance to the complex. Exhibitions have varying requirements; some use turnstiles, some like to register visitors as they enter, others prefer a ticket or badge-only admission system. Most venues have flexible arrangements that can accommodate all of these.

Computer-controlled entry systems will become more wide-spread as Smart cards and related technology develops.

# WORKSHOPS AND STORAGE UNITS

Workshops and storage will be required at many events. They are usually provided because in themselves they are another revenue-producing item for the venue management. At some centres the workshops are large – literally small factories. The contractors and agencies who rent these buildings may be producing standfitting or other services for shows and events all over the UK.

Signwriters, interpreters, temporary staff agencies, florists, exhibition furniture hire companies, newsagents, car rental and theatre ticket agencies are amongst the type of outlets that can be found either in the inside exhibition complex or in the grounds adjoining the entry roads. Venue management know that many people will pass through their property in the course of visiting an exhibition or trade show, and take advantage of the opportunities presented to provide the services that the visitors expect. Catering is another area where the venue can make reasonable profits if good service and value for money are provided, but they must have a busy show – their staff have to be paid even when the complex is empty so it is inevitable that prices will need to be higher to compensate.

The hall and venue owners undertake to provide all these facilities and staff so it can be seen that their initial financial outlay is heavy. They have to amortise these costs over a period of several years and at the same time up-date and maintain the equipment and facilities. They must also pay their staff on a permanent or retained basis although they may only average a 60-65 per cent hall usage by tenants. Some are now increasingly using their buildings for other events such as pop concerts, fashion shows, shareholders' meetings, indoor football and similar events in an effort to increase the profitability of their property.

# OUTSIDE SHOWGROUNDS

A great many outdoor events take place every year, from local village to major county shows. These are mostly based on the agricultural industry but increasingly other trades are taking part in these shows when they can get accepted – for example, household gadgets and DIY tools at agricultural events or clothing and saddlery at horse shows. Such shows attract enthusiastic audiences who may not have the opportunity to travel to the large exhibitions in cities and towns.

Outdoor showgrounds require adequate parking space for exhibitors and visitors and flat and level ground on which to lay out the exhibits. For large shows, purpose-made sites are necessary, with hard pathways, drainage, mains water and waste disposal for restaurants and toilets, and electricity either from a mains supply or by generator. Most major county showgrounds have good facilities and attract large crowds of visitors.

Many of the earlier observations concerning exhibition venue requirements also apply here. The need for the various craft, labour and services is equally great for outside events. Catering facilities can also be very important, particularly in hot summer weather, as anyone who has visited an agricultural show will know.

Major agriculture and county shows will attract the Press in large numbers, so they will require adequate communication systems and a place to work. The Press centre will require facilities to receive Press releases and photographs, display racks, desk space, and all the paraphernalia of the visiting Press corps.

## OTHER VENUES

Exhibitions and shows can be staged in many different venues. Examples include convoys of purpose-built 'fitted' lorries and caravans, which upon arrival at the site (outside is best) can be positioned in the same way that travelling fairground stalls and sideshows are arranged. (Circuses and fairs were the origin of exhibitions; in those days they were called 'goose-fairs'.)

Ships and trains have also been used as travelling exhibition halls. Even a Jumbo jet aircraft has been fitted out as an exhibition setting – a particularly suitable venue if the product has any connection with aircraft. Any vehicle with sufficient space and novelty appeal has the potential for a travelling exhibition venue. In such cases, accommodation for the staff may need to be provided but on a train or ship this is not a problem.

All of these venues have good publicity value and that is part of the requirement. The decision on whether or not to incur the expense of these operations depends very much on the product to be shown.

In all cases it must be remembered that adequate parking has to be provided for staff and visitors and toilets and catering facilities must be nearby. Leisure centres, shopping arcades, sports clubs and race courses have such facilities and are sometimes used as a showbase. They can all be adapted for exhibition use.

Conference-orientated exhibitions are very popular for certain industries. Clearly a conference hall with sufficient seating to accommodate all the expected delegates becomes an essential first requirement. The catering facilities must be sufficient to accommodate the delegates for their meals at the required times, without undue waiting.

New exhibition venues appear every year. Some are very suitable for certain types of shows, but not all. Companies staging their own exhibitions often use these facilities but professional organisers will not usually be interested in venues of less than 2-4000 square metres with the appropriate transportation and communication facilities. The newer hotels are likely to provide the facilities that will correspond to the needs of company-orientated product launches or displays. Many overseas hotels and some of the newer UK hotels are seizing the opportunities now open to them and provide well-planned facilities for such presentations.

## DISADVANTAGED AND DISABLED VISITORS

An increasing number of disabled people are now able to visit exhibitions and trade shows since car manufacturers have recognised the need and are providing suitably adapted transport. Their special needs also have to be considered by venue managements and exhibition organisers.

Specially designated car parking spaces adjoining the entrances are essential. These spaces should be wider than normal to allow wheelchairs to be off-loaded. Disabled people need rather more room when entering or alighting from a car. Healthy visitors should on no account occupy the disabled parking spaces – regrettably this happens all too frequently and not just at exhibitions!

In the building, all entrances and exits should have ramps – it is not easy for the handicapped to use steps and stairs. Ramps should not have a steep incline. Turnstiles and gate entrances should include at least one with wider access for wheelchairs to pass through. Registration points should allow for disabled persons to complete their registration form from a sitting position, often on their lap, since they cannot always easily leave their wheelchair. All toilets should incorporate facilities for the disabled and doors should be wide enough to allow wheelchairs easy access. Doors should not be too heavy to push or pull open – disabled people find this a frequent problem.

Where it is necessary to alter levels in a complex consideration must always be given to the handicapped and ramps provided so that they can have an equal opportunity to tour the whole trade fair or exhibition. Some trade shows exhibit products of particular interest to the disabled. These in particular must ensure easy access to their stands. Platforms are not easy to negotiate for people in wheelchairs or on crutches!

Supermarkets have demonstrated how life for the disabled can be made much easier. Exhibition venues management, organisers and all associated with the industry must ensure they follow their example. In most venues the management is adapting to these standards because as the average age of the population increases, more and more people will need these facilities.

# 11

# TYPES OF EXHIBITION
# ORGANISERS AND THEIR DUTIES

Exhibition organisers generally fall into one of three categories:

- Trade journal publishers diversifying and adding further support to their journals' activities and supplementing advertising revenue in the areas where their name is known. This applies mainly to technical rather than consumer journals.
- Venue owners seeking to fill vacant dates and maximise the venue potential.
- Entrepreneurial companies whose principal business is organising exhibitions and trade fairs.

All of these categories in one way or another make their contribution to the exhibition industry.

## JOURNAL PUBLISHERS

Trade journal publishers are well known in the industries and trades for which they cater. Their journalists and contributors write upon a variety of subjects of interest to the industries they represent. Quite often an industry – particulary one with a new technology – may fragment; as new ideas and technologies develop, another allied subject is born. The computer and software industry is a good example, with so many different developing areas. Each requires its own individual journal, normally spun off by the parent journal. Part of this process of evolution will require that a separate exhibition comes into being.

It is not unknown for the 'fragmented offshoot' to develop into the major event. Examples exist in almost all industries. As new titles evolve old shows must either improve and upgrade their event or close down.

## VENUE OWNERS

As new venues come into being, their own event-organising company follows. Most major exhibition halls and venues have formed their own separate subsidiary company to organise events for their complex. These supplement the bookings achieved from other exhibition organisers. They can range from trade and public exhibitions to sporting events such as boxing matches, tennis squash and badminton, five-a-side football matches, horse shows through to pop concerts and festivals. Television companies quite regularly also use the facilities exhibition halls provide.

Some complexes seek to promote interest in a new type of exhibition or trade fair not currently being staged at that hall or maybe not in that region of the country. A London exhibition may be coveted by a venue in the Midlands or the North, or vice versa, and if the original exhibition organisers cannot be persuaded to duplicate they may endeavour to stage a competing event. There is often a genuine need for a similar exhibition in different areas. Local prospective exhibitors may take this view. In the final analysis, exhibitors will decide by their support, or lack of it!

Venue organisers will often try entirely new ideas for new subjects: some succeed, some fail. Since they do not have to meet the heavy rental guarantees which their clients have to meet, they are in a much better financial situation to do this.

The exhibition industry is highly competitive and if an organiser in any category is complacent, another will quickly replace them. This works to the advantage of the exhibitor; if he is not satisfied, the exhibition will be quickly replaced.

# THE ENTREPRENEUR

Because they are not controlled by outside interests and influences organisers in this category are free to reject any exhibition proposition if in their opinion it is not in the interest of either the visiting buyers or public, or the manufacturers who would be asked to participate. After seeking the views of the prospective trade audience and manufacturing industry, they can provide proposals which are impartial and in keeping with the opinions and views researched from those who would be concerned with the event. Neither trade publishers nor venue interests would be in a position to influence him.

Entrepreneurial organisations are often asked to cooperate with trade associations that wish to stage an exhibition or conference. They can also collaborate with sister bodies overseas, enabling items such as appropriate trade dates to be considered impartially. They often know much about the overseas interests of the industry being examined through their contacts with their opposite members overseas.

Most entrepreneur companies subscribe to the stringent code of conduct laid down by the industry trade association (AEO) to guarantee exhibitors honest and equitable treatment. After an industry has been researched, the resultant answers should satisfy anyone considering such an event. Sometimes the research may indicate the event will not succeed. This they will quantify to their client rather than proceed with a potentially useless exhibition. Any event that profits neither the visiting buyer or the exhibiting manufacturer cannot profit the exhibition organiser either.

Other facilities such as conference organisation and marketing can often be provided by associated divisions of the entrepreneurial companies.

## SPONSORSHIP INFLUENCE

Trade associations, Chambers of Commerce and similar bodies may seek to influence and sometimes cause an exhibition to 'happen'. They may become associated with the exhibition or fair organiser and are publicised as the sponsor of the event. In this role they encourage their members to participate.

## CONSIDERATIONS INVOLVED IN STAGING AN EVENT

Any exhibition or trade fair must satisfy the aims and requirements of the two groups of people involved: first, the attending buyers or visitors, whether trade or public, then the exhibiting companies, in that order – without buyers there is little purpose in the exhibition or its exhibitors. The professional exhibition organiser will ensure that the researchers investigate the opinions of the buyers as well as the manufacturers, to obtain their views on dates and preferred geographical area and the desired frequency of the exhibition. Their opinion on similar events in the UK and overseas will also be sought. Such research takes time and can be costly but at the end of the day an honest survey will result in a useful mailing list containing some thousand or more important names (depending on the size of the industry) for possible future use. Direct mail houses can sometimes provide an initial list but the experienced exhibition organiser will use them as an aid rather than a total list. Trade journal publishers usually have good lists but they are often reluctant to divulge them to competitive interests, unless they were the sponsors of a particular event.

Mailed questionnaires are but a start. Useful as they are, they do not provide the shades of opinion that are required. This is done by the telephone interviewer, who is often also experienced in telephone sales. Two objectives can be achieved: an opinion, and if this is supportive, a tentative space reservation or buyer's ticket request. The opinions can provide the basis of the initial approach to a group of potential exhibitors or manufacturers who could then be sent a preliminary sales brochure. Alternatively, the important buyers within an industry may be sent an initial visitor information pack.

One of the consequences of the opinion survey is that people in a particular industry will start talking, which in itself will have a snowball effect and help discussion with future potential clients. The seasoned exhibitor will quickly recognise whether or not an event has been competently researched and is worthy of serious consideration. If, however, the research indicates the event should not take place, this saves the visitor, exhibitor and organiser both money and time.

## INFORMING AND SERVICING THE EXHIBITOR

Having decided to proceed with the exhibition, the organiser must confirm the hall reservation – which he will have tentatively booked – since all venues plan their schedules many months, sometimes years ahead. The promotional literature must be prepared and published and mailed to all concerned. It is always useful to send initial early information to the visitors as well since the exhibition depends upon them. Press releases need preparing and continuing stories should be despatched to trade journals at periodic intervals so that an exhibition rhetoric is established.

If the event aims to attract overseas buyers, appropriate press stories and publicity must be circulated to the overseas trade journals. Press releases can also be usefully sent to the British trade consulates overseas with a request to bring it to the attention of local trade associations. Most organisers will ensure that their press department and publicity people contact overseas groups early in the day, and it is often possible to obtain joint venture group exhibits from various countries.

As the space salespeople achieve their space sales, application forms and floor plans have to be sent to all exhibitors together with details of the services that are available and the rules and regulations governing the exhibitors' participation. Most of these are imposed upon the exhibition organiser, who has a duty to inform the exhibitor, as we discussed earlier. The exhibitor's manual also has to be prepared at this stage. As well as servicing the exhibitors the organising team also have to liaise with the ancillary trades and professions involved in the exhibition on behalf of various exhibitors. These will include designers, architects, advertising agencies, PR consultants, shipping agents from overseas as well as the UK and all the other statutory authorities. This is the time that organisers' staff really get to know their exhibitors.

Most organisers issue lists of exhibitors at periodic intervals for circulation to interested buyers and the press. Notification of any special visits to the event are updated in exhibitor information sheets. The exhibitor should also inform the organiser of any events they are arranging so that the maximum benefit can be obtained through joint publicity efforts.

Some organisers hold briefing meetings in convenient centres where question and answer sessions can clarify any obscure points. Inexperienced and new exhibitors find such sessions useful, and they also meet other exhibitors.

## THE SITE BUILD-UP

The organiser or hall surveyor is responsible for marking out the hall to correspond with the floor plan that has been issued to those concerned with the exhibition or trade fair. All stand building contractors will work strictly to this plan. (We dealt with this at some length in Chapter 7.) It is worth emphasising again that aisles and gangways must be kept as clear as possible during the build-up and to remember that all exhibitors and contractors can use only their own stand space to deposit materials. The stand numbers will be written on the floor of the hall, usually by chalked-out stand dividing lines.

The organiser's exhibition manager is all-powerful during the period that the exhibition is on the floor. It is his or her job to ensure that the traffic and personnel movements of everyone – exhibitor, builder and organising staff, whether inside the hall or on the outside approaches – proceeds in an orderly manner without impeding any other person. The off-loading of exhibits onto a stand must always be completed as quickly as possible and vehicles cleared from the hall to make space for others.

Security personnel must keep strict control over all entrances, exit gates and doors. The need for security officers increases as opening day nears and more and more exhibits arrive on stands. All the time the organiser's exhibition manager and staff must be watching for exhibitors or stand fitters who do not appear to be making realistic progress and may be unlikely to be ready for the opening day. The district surveyor will withhold permission to open to visitors if the exhibition hall is not entirely clear and safe to his satisfaction.

Any damage to the hall or floor must be noted as it arises; it could become the subject of a claim by the venue owner. Mains connections by the hall engineers must be made by the stated time.

## THE OPEN PERIOD

If the preparatory work has been done properly the actual trade show time should be routine. Any celebrities and VIPs will make their appearance and be shown around the exhibition. Television and radio crews and media journalists will be touring the event; the Press centre will be busy answering questions. At a successful trade show new intending exhibitors will at this time be asking for stands at the next event and existing exhibitors may wish to improve the stand position they have.

## CHILDREN'S CRECHES AT PUBLIC EVENTS

It is always helpful, especially with public shows, to provide a children's creche within the exhibition, complete with toys and children's amusements and, of course, qualified staff. Various manufacturers are interested in sponsoring this type of activity (it links with their type of business and provides good publicity). Professional organisations exist to carry out the task of baby minding with nurses and specialist staff.

## CATERING

Catering can often be dificult at the busy periods, particularly if several private parties are on at the same time together perhaps with an opening luncheon. However, exhibition catering teams at the major venues can rapidly move great numbers of people through their cafeterias and restaurants.

## EMERGENCY SERVICES

First aid facilities must be available at all venues. In the larger complexes, nursing sisters are available and a doctor will be on call. At large shows where maybe several hundred workmen are building, accidents are inevitable. All exhibition organisers can quote cases of every description, from broken limbs and heart attacks to babies being born! Organising personnel should know where the first aid, fire office and security are located.

# THE BREAKDOWN AND CLEARING

Because of increasing hall costs, breakdown periods are getting shorter. They usually start on the closing night of the show. Exhibitors should clear their lighter products away quickly to minimise the problem of traffic congestion on the outside approaches of the exhibition complex, particularly after a large trade show. Very strict stewardship is necessary if these problems are to be avoided. Where public highways are involved, the police should be consulted and, if necessary, extra staff and stewards employed. This is always the time that poses a great security risk for any loose products which happen to be lying around.

The actual breakdown inside the hall moves at a fast rate once all the products are away, and usually starts early on the morning following the end of the show. All sites need to be checked for damage as they are vacated, and contractors' vehicles should be watched as they pass through some of the more narrow opening doors and exits, particularly at the older halls. Gatemen must be aware of the potential hazard. Any damage to the hall fabric is the responsibility of the occupying tenant, the exhibitor or the builder.

Exhibitors and their builders are required to leave their stand space absolutely clear. Quite often they do not clear carpet tape from the floor, a job which is very time-consuming and, if not done, will be charged to the tenant (the organiser) by the hall owner. This particular item is probably the most common of all hall delapidations and one that causes the greatest annoyance to organisers and venue management.

The final job the exhibition manager performs is to carry out the final hall inspection in the company of the hall management's representative in order to obtain his signature for a 'clean hall'.

## ORGANISERS' INQUEST

In an earlier chapter we looked at the advantages and disadvantages of the actual stand so that the exhibitor could improve the performance the next time around. This inquest is for the benefit of the organiser: how can he provide a better show next time?

Some organisers ask their exhibitors to complete a written questionnaire. Others rely on exhibitors' letters or comments made to their staff. In any case, the organisers' staff should be required to attend a staff meeting where any problems can be discussed. Any shortcomings and good ideas should be noted for future events. It is useful to do this quite soon after the event, certainly no later than a month after. If it is an annual show a second meeting, say about two months later, might be useful to establish guidelines for the next event in the series.

# 12

# LOOKING AHEAD – WHO CAN HELP?

It is not always realised how many people other than those directly involved contribute to the success of exhibitions and trade fairs. For example, many exhibitors who employ advertising agencies will first turn to them for advice; since they provide general marketing and publicity expertise, it is natural to seek their opinion and help on exhibitions and trade fairs.

Most advertising agencies have a competent working knowledge of the exhibition industry. Many have their own exhibition departments who are in regular contact with organisers and exhibition designers. They also work at the various venues from time to time and employ stand contractors. Those who do not have such a department will have established working relations with the appropriate experts. How comprehensive their service is and the extent of work they can carry out will need to be established – it will vary from agency to agency. The cost of such a service is a further determining factor. This also varies and it has to be accepted there are good and bad operators. In an ideal situation, when preparing his client's yearly publicity and promotional plan, the exhibitor's advertising agency will have foreseen the need to incorporate the exhibition or trade fair just as it should have foreseen any trade journal or media advertising. This should have been included in the recommendations and budget projection. In the case of a consumer client, the exhibition planning together with the styling of the exhibition stand would be expected to closely reflect the creative thinking of any TV commercials and Sunday newspaper magazine copy. Unfortunately some agencies often see their task as advising only on newspaper, journal, TV and radio advertising. With extensive television broadcasting via satellite and cable links attracting enormous viewing figures, it is all too easy to put such media at the top of the list. The problem is that a great many people regard TV commercial breaks as a nuisance. Furthermore, how many people whose business is technical will be attracted by this medium for advertising? The question which should be uppermost in every advertiser's mind at all times when considering promotion of any type is 'Will it attract my type of buyer?'

Agencies should also be able to assist in the preparation of the brief and advise on specialist events which could be beneficial to the client. They should advise on the choice of designers or architects and, ultimately, on suitable standfitting specialists. The agency programme should start with the brief and progress to any publicity and marketing requirements such as photography, product brochures, posters and the many detailed items that make up the exhibition project. They need to work closely with the appointed exhibition manager.

Matters like hotel bookings, temporary staff, catering and similar items are probably best handled by the exhibition manager. If an advertising agency has an all-embracing exhibition department they may possibly undertake the total operation. The cost of such a service will usually be quoted separately but in some cases it may be included in the agency's overall service fee. If the advertising agency does not carry out this work several other options are available, as described below.

# EXHIBITION CONSULTANTS

Consultants may work for a specialist company or as freelance operators. In either case they should be able to handle all the necessary details. Most have long experience through working in one or more of the exhibition activities. If required, they can perform the duties of an exhibition manager. They will provide a written quotation detailing the services they can offer and stating the level of effort they will provide (i.e. the amount of time to be spent on inspection in the standfitters' works, the amount of site supervision to be provided and details on dismantling).

If a consultant has several commissions at the same event, site time can be shared with other stand-holders at the same exhibition, if all are agreeable, and this can reduce expenditure. However, if he has undertaken other duties at a show it would not be wise to employ him as an exhibition manager – this requires unlimited attention.

# PR CONSULTANTS

Public relations consultants have become more active in the exhibition business, performing much the same function as advertising agencies. This is not surprising since successful exhibition stands, particularly at the public shows, depend greatly on the impact and interest they create, and it is the energetic exhibition PR executive who creates that impact. Those who specialise in exhibition promotion work closely with exhibition designers and others and their contribution to the exhibition brief becomes important.

# STANDFITTERS

Many standfitters will also provide other services in addition to performing their major building role. They can provide designs and drawings (which remain their copyright), the cost of which will then be included in the quotation for the complete stand work they will supply. Their designs obviously cannot be submitted to tender with other standfitters, as could be done with a freelance designer's work which the exhibitor has commissioned. For smaller exhibition projects this an effective method of working. Frequent exhibitors who are using shell schemes find it economical.

## DECIDING – WHICH IS BEST?

As might be expected, whichever method is used there will inevitably be a bias toward the favoured area of the originator. The designer will follow a design bias while the PR person will be striving for a newsworthy angle. The advertising agent may be leading into a publicity tie-up with the media, while the standfitter may want to use a particular structure or materials to prove his ability or because he foresees a future use for such elements. All of these will have a particular axe to grind, but does this matter? The exhibitor wants a good and attractive stand. If the chosen person achieves that the effort will have been worth while. As in all other promotional work, the executive who is controlling the project – usually the exhibition manager – must decide what is to be done and how much the supplier's enthusiasm is to be encouraged or restrained.

If the exhibition is a small regional affair which the local sales manager has handled successfully for a number of years, it can possibly be improved by evaluating past costs and results and setting new achievement targets. If it is a small but major new trade show likely to attract many important clients and it is known that your principal competitors will figure strongly, it is advisable to have a senior publicity or marketing manager to handle it for your company and employ good professionals to handle participation details.

# THE FUTURE – WHAT NEXT?

In today's economic and political climate it is difficult to foresee the direction that marketing or advertising efforts might take. If one looks at history, however, it is apparent that exhibitions and trade fairs have played a significant role in promoting and marketing products or services ever since The Great Exhibition of 1851 at Crystal Palace in London, which was probably the forerunner of the large spectacular exhibition or trade fairs that we know today. Indeed, this event was quickly followed by the New York World Fair in 1853 and the Exposition Universelle in Paris in 1889, when the Eiffel Tower was built. Chicago followed in 1893 – the trend was developing.

The last 'spectacular' – the 1992 Expo at Seville – indicates the success of such events in drawing attention to a country and its products. These fairs have become increasingly international with many countries being represented. Particularly noticeable are the newcomers from the Third World. Perhaps more significantly, important buyers and trade ministers appear to be taking greater notice of these events and their participants. The trend shows every sign of continuing as newer trading areas attract more interest and become more important.

# THE INFLUENCE OF EXHIBITIONS AND TRADE SHOWS

The European Union, with its aim of monetary union by 1999, is encouraging greater inter-trading between member countries, though this may not always be to the members' advantage. Manufacturers from the Asian/Pacific Rim areas are also developing very fast and because they do not have many large trade fairs in their own countries, they are taking advantage of the fairs held in Europe and the USA.

The latest figures available indicate that Japan, Asian and Pacific rim manufacturers of products such as consumer electronic equipment and motor vehicles have increased their participation as exhibitors in European trade fairs by something like 8 per cent in 1992/3. (Figures for 1994 were not available at the time of writing, but this trend is probably being maintained.) Their attendance as visitors also continues to increase, as it has done for many years. Importers from the country staging the trade show can benefit from this situation since they have the opportunity to acquire the agencies for these Eastern manufacturers. Consumer electronics and motor industry trade shows in mainland Europe are amongst the largest trade events and the biggest exhibitors are from Japan and the Pacific rim countries. Unfortunately, the UK does not appear to have an answer and currently does not stage a large trade fair for consumer electronics.

The one-to-one sales approach provided at exhibitions and trade fairs will always provide a much greater sales conversion rate than other media options. Something like 700 to 1000 UK exhibitions and trade fairs are listed in the *Exhibition Bulletin* annually and it is likely that the majority of these are trade rather than public events. On average, such trade events run for four or five days.

Depending on the subject, a major trade show at a mainline venue will attract up to 2000 or more people per day. If only half that number attended a five-day major trade show this would therefore represent 5000 people, all of whom have an interest or could become interested in the products on display. No other media can create this face-to-face interest for trade products – trade journals can show pictures but cannot provide the opportunity of touching or operating the product.

## FIGURES AND TRENDS

The Incorporated Society of British Advertisers (ISBA) produces a yearly survey of exhibition expenditure by UK companies and I am indebted to them for permission to use these figures.

In 1992 (the latest figures available), £519 million was spent on exhibitions in the UK. This compares with £539 million spent in 1991. Significantly, however, these figures do not include expenditure on private and agricultural exhibitions, which were greater in 1992 than in 1991.

It is also significant that more exhibitors used shell schemes, particularly the modular type. Some also purchased their own modular stands and components and this had the effect of reducing the exhibitors' expenditure on standfitting. This implies that the apparent drop in expenditure was not that great but the recession obviously did have some effect.

# POSSIBLE NEW MARKETS

Overall, the amount spent by British companies exhibiting overseas in 1992 was £246 million, which compares to £281 million in 1991. Of this, 61 per cent was spent on events in the European Union. A total of 75 per cent was spent on direct participation, while 25 per cent was spent with the DTI Joint Venture Trade Fair Support scheme. Asia represented 5.3 per cent of the expenditure and North America almost 12 per cent.

Although the Latin American markets also offer trading opportunities, the British participation via trade fairs is small. The former Soviet nations and Eastern European countries have hardly been considered as yet though they have a great requirement for capital plant and equipment. What easier way to demonstrate and sell capital equipment in such areas than by taking it to the potential buyer via a trade fair? It saves the expense of travelling, and if several exporting companies mounted their own joint venture with shared shipping and standfitting, the costs would be reduced. Trade associations can approach the DTI Overseas Promotions Support Scheme and ask for Joint Venture Aid. Problems associated with payment are well-known but they can often be overcome by using barter deals and many companies are already doing this.

The area that offers the greatest potential for export has to be found by each individual company. Visits and fact-finding missions should be carried out by senior executives of the company. We live in a fast-changing world and those who wish to survive and grow must recognise that if they do not export to often unfamiliar markets they will face increasing competition from those companies and countries who are prepared to do so. Japanese and German companies have already demonstrated their determination in this direction. The International Motor show used to be a predominantly British show; it is still held in the UK but now it is mainly an overseas market place, using a British trade show to promote overseas products!

## INFORMATION SOURCES

The Department of Trade Export Market Information Centre, local Chambers of Commerce and High Street banks should all be able to provide facts and figures on most markets. The Department of Trade and Industry (DTI) already have joint ventures for many overseas exhibitions and the trade association for particular industries should be able to provide help and information.

## WHAT IS TO COME IN THE FUTURE?

Modular exhibitions will increase in popularity – any method that reduces costs will be readily accepted. Presentation methods will change as new technology develops. The exhibition industry has always been innovative and will always be in the forefront of any new development. 'Projected' exhibitions via satellite and computer links through fibre optics are being developed, and video conferencing is becoming more commonplace. Who can say how far these will develop? They have the disadvantage, however, that they do not provide the all important 'people factor', where buyers and sellers can intermingle, make new business contacts, compare notes and socialise. This has always been the great advantage that trade fairs have over the printed and projected news media. People are social creatures and like to compare notes and gossip – in itself this creates business opportunities.

The advantages, however, are readily seen by companies wishing to communicate at long distances – for example, UK companies negotiating with buyers in Singapore or USA can save valuable time and demonstrate machinery products on video screens and via fax and voice links they can discuss products without long journey times travelling to their business contacts. Specialised companies are developing these techniques which will become more widely available in the future, though at present they are still expensive.

With the evolution of 'smart cards' and touchscreens future buyers will be able to establish immediate contact with the seller and conduct meaningful negotiations. The problems of time differences will be a challenge, however.

Laser, holograph, computer and specialised software suppliers have already contributed interesting ideas to exhibition presentations and since in many cases they are only at the beginning of their development we can expect further features from them. Theatrical techniques are becoming increasingly interwoven with exhibition and trade fair presentations, and major exhibition venues like the National Exhibition Centre, Earls Court and Olympia are staging an increasing number of other events like pop concerts, opera, ice shows, horse shows, etc. Their builders and designers could well suggest to their trade fair and exhibition clients that these various theatrical ideas could also attract additional interest to their stands.

The exhibition industry has expanded considerably throughout the world over the last two decades. Though some stand-building companies and other suppliers experienced difficult trading conditions in the UK in the late eighties and early nineties, on the world scene more exhibition halls have been built and are still being built. Existing venues are being extended – as at the NEC Birmingham and Earls Court London – more hotels are developing exhibition facilities within their complexes, particularly in the Far East, and more trade show titles have come into being.

*The British Pavilion at Expo 92 in Seville, Spain.*

# APPENDIX 1

# SOME UK EXHIBITION AND CONFERENCE CENTRES

Aberdeen Exhibition and Conference Centre, Aberdeen (tel. 01224-824824)

Alexandra Palace, London (tel. 0181-365 2121)

Barbican Centre, London (tel. 0171-638 4141)

Brighton Conference Centre, Brighton (tel. 01273-21173)

Bristol Exhibition Centre, Bristol (tel. 0117-9298630)

Bournemouth International Centre, Bournemouth (tel. 01202-558841)

Business Design Centre, London (tel. 0171-359 3535)

Castle Donington Exhibition Centre, Derby (tel. 01332-812919)

Doncaster Exhibition Centre, Doncaster (tel. 01302- 320066)

Earls Court, London (tel. 0171 370- 8003)

Edinburgh Exhibition and Trade Centre, Edinburgh (tel. 0131-333 3036)

G-Mex Centre, Manchester (tel. 0161- 834 2700)

Harrogate International Centre, Harrogate (tel. 01423-500 500)

Kings Hall, Belfast (tel. 01232- 665225)

Metropole Exhibition Hall, Brighton (tel. 01273- 775432)

National Agricultural Centre, Stoneleigh (tel. 01203-535711)
National Exhibition Centre, Birmingham (tel. 0121-780 4141)
Olympia Conference and Exhibition Centre, London (tel. 0171-370 8400)
Royal Horticultural Halls, London (tel. 0171-834 4333)
Sandown Exhibition Centre, Esher (tel. 01372-467540)
Scottish Exhibition and Conference Centre, Glasgow (tel. 0141-248 3000)
Telford Exhibition Centre, Telford (tel. 01952-291199)
Wembley Centre, Wembley (tel. 0181-902 8833)
Winter Gardens, Blackpool (tel. 01253-25252)

# APPENDIX 2

# USEFUL ADDRESSES

Advertising Association
3 Crawford Place
London W1H 1JB
0171-723 8028

Advertising Standards Authority
Brook House
Torringdon Place
London WC1E 7HN
0171-580 5555

Association of Exhibition Organisers
26 Chapter Street
London SW1T 4ND
0171-932 0252

Association of International Courier and Express Services
PO Box 10
Leatherhead
Surrey KT22 OHT
01372-284 2953

British Exporters Association
16 Dartmouth Street
London SW1H 9BL
0171-222 5419

British Exhibition Contractors Association
Kingsmere House
Graham Road
Wimbledon
London SW19 3SR
0181-543 3888

British Institute of Management
2 Savoy Court
Strand
London WC2R OEZ
0171-497 0580

British International Freight Association
Redfern House
Browells Lane
Fetham
Middlx TWI3 7EP
0181-844 2266

British Standards Institute
2 Park Street
London WIA 2BS
0171-629 9000

Chartered Institute of Marketing
Moor Hall
Cookham
Maidenhead
Berkshire SL6 9QH
01628-524922

Chartered Society of Designers
29 Bedford Square
London WCl 3EG
0171-631 1510

Department of Trade and Industry
Export Publications
PO BOX 55
Stratford on Avon
Warwickshire CV37 9GE
01789-296212

Department of Trade and Industry
Overseas Promotions Support
Dean Bradley House
Horseferry Road
London SW1P 2AG
0171-276 2414

Design Council
28 Haymarket
London SW1Y 4SU
0171-839 8000

*Exhibition Bulletin*
266-272 Kirkdale
London SE26 4RZ
0181-778 2288

Exports Buying Offices Association
c/o Portman Ltd
360 Oxford Street
London WlA 4BY
0171-493 8141

Exports Credits Guarantee Department
2 Exchange Tower
PO Box 2200
Harbour Exchange
London E14 9GS
0171-512 7000

Incorporated Society of British Advertisers
44 Hereford Street
London W1Y 8AE
0171-499 7502

Institute of Export
Export House
64 Clifton Street
London EC2A 4HB
0171-247 9812

International Chamber of Commerce
14-15 Belgrave Square
London SW1X 8PS
0171-823 2811

Royal Society of Arts
8 John Adam Street
London WC2N 6EZ
0171-930 5115

Technical Help To Exporters
Linford Wood
Milton Keynes
MK14 6LE
01908-220022

Union des Foires Internationales
35 Rue Jouffroy
Paris 75017
France
(010 33 1) 42-67-99-12

# APPENDIX 3

# SERVICES FOR UK EXPORTERS

The Department of Trade through their Overseas Trade Services provides a wide range of useful services to UK exporters. For the benefit of those companies new to exporting, these are briefly noted here. Full details and explanatory literature is available through the DTI's offices located around the UK. Overseas, they have a worldwide network.

The Enterprise Initiative. Consultancy help for companies employing fewer than 500 people.

Export Data Services. Provision of an export marketing information service with databases, statistics, market reports and directories.

Export Representation. Assisting in the appointment of overseas representatives.

Trade Fairs Support Scheme. Assistance in exhibiting overseas, including financial grants towards space and standfitting costs.

Inward Missions. Financial support to bring influential overseas buyers to UK product-related events.

Outward Missions. Support offered to exporters to fact-find 'first-hand' as part of a trade group.

A range of publications is also available, including profiles of countries. In 1990/91 the DTI spent around £166m on support for exporters including Foreign Office costs overseas. They support around 6600 participants in overseas trade fairs each year. Over 1700 participants used the Outward Missions service in 1990/91. (Information provided by the Department of Trade and Industry.) Enquiries tel. 0171-215 5000, Fax 0171-828 3258)

# INDEX

# How to Maximise Exhibition Sales
## Proven techniques for sales success
### Sales Booster Audio Cassette

*(Cassette; £9.99, 1-85252-170-0)*

The chances are, you'll generate a number of leads at your next exhibition. But could you have done more? And will you get the best out of the ones you did obtain?

This cassette will give you two clear plans – one for the exhibition itself, and one for the follow-up period.

Exhibitions are expensive; make sure you get your full value out of them.

**'Very effective ... a valuable supplement to both formal and field training.'** F J Smart, Training Services Manager, Toshiba

Also on this audio-cassette: *How to Improve Business from Telephone Enquiries.*

Sales Booster Audio Cassettes are the perfect way to improve sales skills. The travelling salesman can simply listen to the cassette as he travels to his next appointment. Other titles in the series include:

*How to make telephone appointments every time.*
*How to make sure you close the sale every time.*
*Selling to bigger companies.*
*How to sell effectively on the telephone.*
*How to avoid negative thinking.*
*How to handle discount requests.*
*A new look at objection handling*
*How to overcome the money objection.*
*'I could never be a salesman'.*